The Doctor's Guide to Protecting Your Health Before, During and After International Travel

January 2, 2001

Happy Birthday
Yvonne

Love always,
Mom
XO

the *well-prepared traveler* series

The Doctor's Guide to Protecting Your Health Before, During and After International Travel

by
W. Robert Lange, M.D., M.P.H.

pilot books

PILOT BOOKS
127 Sterling Avenue
Greenport, New York 11944

1997 Edition

Library of Congress Catalog Card Number: 97-17148

Library of Congress Cataloging in Publication Data

Lange, W. Robert.
The doctor's guide to protecting your health before, during and after international travel / by W. Robert Lange.
p. cm. - (well-prepared traveler series)
Previous ed. published with title: The international health guide for senior citizen travelers.
Includes bibliographical references and index.
ISBN 0-87576-209-3 (alk. paper)
1. Travel--Health aspects. 2. Aged--Travel--Health aspects.
I. Lange, W. Robert. International health guide for senior citizen travelers.
II. Title. III. Series.
RA783.5.L357 1997
613.6'8--dc21 97-17148
CIP

Printed in the United States of America

About the author

W. Robert Lange, M.D. M.P.H. earned his M.D. degree from the Medical College of Wisconsin and completed his postgraduate medical training at Johns Hopkins and its affiliated hospitals. He is Board Certified in both Internal Medicine and Preventive Medicine Public Health. Much of his clinical practice is devoted to bridging those two areas, including adult immunization and other infectious disease prevention strategies.

Dr. Lange has published articles on travel health matters in both medical journals and consumer publications. He regularly conducts travel medicine educational programs for physicians in practice and helped establish the Travel Medicine Clinic at Hopkins Hospital. His research interests include the toxic and infectious hazards of travel.

Contents

Introduction

People travel internationally for many reasons. One - especially for today's older adult - is to improve one's health. Whether recuperating from an illness or traveling as a form of preventive medicine, taking a trip abroad can have a rejuvenating, healing effect on the mind and body.

Unfortunately, international travel also imposes certain health risks. Surprisingly, a nationwide survey of state health departments showed that **most international travelers are inadequately or inappropriately informed about travel health matters and approximately one traveler in four will experience at least one illness while abroad.**

This book is intended to help both seasoned and less experienced travelers. It identifies potential health risks and hazards which could occur underway, abroad, or after returning home and describes what's important to address during the pre-departure planning phase. Although the information in this volume applies to all travelers, it pinpoints, highlights, and emphasizes the unique concerns of senior travelers.

Not only are older adults traveling more, but the nature and complexity of their travel is also evolving. Some are more likely to venture off the beaten path and, in the process, encountering new medical risks and issues. More are staying abroad longer, while others are actually retiring overseas. This edition includes specific advice on topics from adventure travel to retirement abroad.

Since the first edition of this book (then called The International Health Guide for Senior Citizen Travelers) was published almost ten years ago, much has changed on the global health and travel scenes. From the perspective of infectious diseases, some conditions have become less of a problem. Polio, for example has essentially been eradicated from the Western Hemisphere.

Other infectious conditions, however, have evolved. The AIDS epidemic is still very much with us unfortunately and, since an individual's risk for this condition may be affected by certain behaviors associated with international travel, travelers require specific information and preparation regarding AIDS. In recent years, new infections have come on the global scene, such as Ebola Zaire. Consequently, this Second Edition contains expanded infectious disease coverage, including a detailed update on AIDS-related issues.

Over the past ten years, the very act of preparing for overseas travel has also changed. The widespread availability of the personal computer, along with the growing popularity of "surfing the net", has made it easy to access a wealth of travel information. There are a number of web sites specific to travel medicine and international health issues. This edition includes an up-to-date listing of selected internet sites that can be of considerable benefit in planning and preparing for an international junket.

Chapter One

Planning to Stay Healthy Abroad

The success of any venture depends on appropriate planning and preparation and this certainly holds true for international travel. **Americans are traveling overseas in record numbers and, each year, well in excess of one-half million of us need a doctor or require hospitalization while abroad.** Certainly not all of these illnesses and injuries could have been prevented by a visit to the family physician before departure, but many of them could. In the process, considerable expense and inconvenience might have been avoided. It is, therefore, prudent to visit your doctor as part of your preparations for an international vacation.

Of course not every overseas visit requires a doctor's visit. Obviously, a month in Tibet needs more preparation and planning than a weekend in Toronto. Generally, however, a visit, or at least a phone call, should be considered in the following circumstances:

- You have underlying medical conditions which require periodic follow-up or regular therapy.
- You'll be visiting less developed areas of the world or your travel itinerary takes you off the beaten path.
- The trip will mean being overseas in excess of 3-4 weeks.

When some medical assessment is needed before going abroad, it's important to plan ahead so there's enough time for all that might be required. **Medical preparation should begin two to three months prior to scheduled departure so there's time for:**

- Scheduling all necessary appointments
- Obtaining all required immunizations
- Being evaluated and treated for any existing problems
- Procuring any necessary medical supplies for the trip

Many physicians do the following to assess a patient prior to a far-flung overseas escapade:

- Obtain an updated medical history.
- Review the trip itinerary to assure the agenda is reasonable, given the unique health profile of the traveler, and ascertain whether or not any unique precautions are advisable.
- Perform a physical examination.
- Arrange for appropriate laboratory testing, including chest x-rays, cardiograms, and TB skin testing, when indicated.
- Plan the immunization schedule and determine whether or not malaria will be a risk. The pre-departure visits are an opportune time to catch-up or remain current with routine immunization needs, including influenza vaccine, the pneumococcal vaccine, and a tetanus-diphtheria booster.
- Address any complaints or minor medical conditions.

A comprehensive evaluation before departure is invaluable for many reasons. It allows your (or another) doctor to compare your state of health before your trip with your health status at the end of the trip, or sooner, should an unexpected need arise. Also, minor medical problems are much better attended to prior to departure than after arrival in a foreign locale. Not only might the condition worsen in transit but, once overseas, the traveler's medical history will be unknown, and cultural and language obstacles may interfere with your receiving proper care.

You may begin to receive immunizations during the first visit. The timing of any follow-up visit(s) will depend upon the nature of the trip, the number of immunizations required and time available.

During the pre-departure, planning phase, find out whether your trip will include travel within regions where malaria and yellow fever might be a threat. If malaria is a risk, it's important to discuss malaria prevention (prophylaxis) and obtain prescriptions for the necessary drugs. Yellow fever vaccine needs to be administered at special vaccination centers and many only provide the inoculation one or two days per week. Be sure to allow enough time, pre-departure, for getting an appointment, if this protection is required.

While discussing the upcoming trip with your family doctor, get prescriptions for any medications you might need while traveling, those you normally take as well as special items for the take-along medical kit. Obtain extra prescriptions for the important drugs and, since they may need to be filled at an overseas pharmacy, **it is very important that they be written legibly using the generic name of the medication.** As a general rule, however, try to take along sufficient medication to last for the duration of the trip. **One cannot count on the universal availability of many of the medications that have become commonplace within this country.**

Once your pre-departure health assessment is completed, ask your doctor for a signed statement on his or her letterhead indicating the date of the examination and that you were found to be in good health and free of contagious disease. If there are any chronic medical conditions, and if medications (particularly controlled substances) are taken on a regularly prescribed basis, this information should be included. Make several photocopies of this statement in case the original is lost or a copy is requested overseas. While on the subject of pharmaceuticals, remember customs officials in foreign countries check prescriptions carefully, and a doctor's certificate should be specific if you need to travel with medications that are controlled and/or potentially abusable. Also, **it is very important that medications be transported in their original containers with labels intact.**

Dental Evaluation

A visit to the family dentist before you leave is also a good idea. Surveys conducted by the Public Health Service and clinicians working in the field of travel medicine, have consistently shown that **tooth and gum problems tend to be among the more common health-related complaints experienced by international travelers.** All cavities should be treated before traveling abroad, and all existing restorations examined to assure their integrity. Furthermore, all potential problems should be taken care of before you leave. In many areas of the world dentists are a scarce commodity, and, all too often, the only treatment for any dental complaint is extraction.

Approximately 20 million Americans wear false teeth, and if you're in the process of being fitted with dentures, you should postpone travel plans until there is a correct fit and accommodation to the dental appliance. As long as there is pain and irritation, stay near home. For the stable denture wearer, travel is no problem, but regular cleansing of the dentures with water from a safe source is important. It might be fruitful to review extensive travel itineraries with your family dentist as you did with the family doctor. This is particularly true if you're remaining overseas for an extended period. Your dentist may be able to give you referrals for dental practitioners near the destinations you plan to visit or reside in for a time. This could be quite helpful if you have dental difficulties while underway. If it is not possible to get a provider's name, try to learn the location of the closest dental school to your destination.

First Aid Kit for Travelers

Many travelers find it reassuring to pack a small medical kit. The contents, of course, will vary according to your preferences, your destination and how long you'll be traveling. The items listed below should enable you to deal with a variety of common minor problems and mishaps. While you may choose to take along more or fewer items, the appropriateness of any prescription medications must be made with input from your personal physician.

Examples of what you should probably include in your kit are: an antihistamine which is an effective anti-allergy preparation; a remedy for motion sickness; and an effective, yet safe, sleeping aid. An even stronger anti-motion sickness preparation may be needed by a few. Anti-diarrheal agents should be taken along, but not used indiscriminately. You may be glad you have them available, however, before an extended tour or a long plane trip home.

TABLE ~ MEDICAL KIT

Nonmedicinal Items

Cotton balls and swabs
Gauze pads (2x2, 4x4)
Roll bandages
Adhesive strip bandages, assorted sizes
Adhesive tape
Scissors
Tweezers and/or hemostat
Soap/disinfectant
Cotton elastic (e.g. Ace bandage)
Safety pins
Dental floss
Insect repellent
Insect netting, if appropriate
Alcohol wipes
Thermometer
Sunglasses

Nonprescription Drugs

Aspirin or acetaminophen (e.g. Tylenol)
Suntan lotion and/or sunscreen
Antihistamine (e.g. Benadryl)
Anti-diarrheal agent (e.g. Imodium AD)
Lip balm
Skin lubricant
Antacid (tablets easier to transport than liquid)
Mild laxative (for Travelers' Constipation)
Hemorrhoidal suppositories, if appropriate
Antimicrobial skin ointment
Water purification supplies, if appropriate
A mild decongestant (if not contraindicated)
Topical steroid cream
Bismuth subsalicylate tablets (Pepto Bismol)

Prescription Medications

Regularly prescribed (maintenance) medications
Special drugs prescribed on an individual basis
Prescription for severe motion sickness, if appropriate
Antimalarial prophylaxis, if indicated
Antibiotic for treatment of severe travelers' diarrhea

Ophthalmologic Preparation

If you have acute eye symptoms or chronic visual problems, you should probably see your eye doctor before going abroad. Anyone venturing overseas for a year or longer should certainly schedule a visit.

Generally, the following visual accessories should be packed:

- A second pair of current prescription glasses, if available.
- At least one pair of sunglasses, polarizing type. Those who wear prescription lenses should give serious consideration to purchasing prescription sunglasses.
- A copy of the lens prescription.
- For contact lens wearers: two pair of contacts, a copy of the prescription, a quality pair of sunglasses and an ample supply of wetting and cleaning solutions.

Resource Organizations

There are a variety of organizations that offer the traveling public a wealth of helpful information, there is a list of these in the Appendix. Some warrant specific comment. Serious travelers should be familiar with the International Association for Medical Assistance to Travelers (IAMAT). This non-profit organization can provide the following helpful material:

- World Immunization Chart
- World Climate Charts
- Passport-size Clinical Record
- Guidelines for adjusting to heat and altitude
- Specific information on the risks and protective strategies for selected infectious diseases:
    - Malaria
    - Schistosomiasis
- A directory of English speaking physicians in cities around the world who will:
    - Have an acceptable degree of competency
    - Abide by a predetermined fee schedule
    - Be readily accessible

Services of IAMAT are free, but donations are welcome.

Several organizations specialize in providing succinct, comprehensive medical records that are convenient to take when traveling. One such firm is the Medical Passport Foundation, a non-profit organization which publishes a document in which pertinent medical information can be summarized.

It is particularly important for international travelers to carry special identification if certain critical situations exist regarding health. People with various medical problems, including allergies, should wear a medical alert bracelet or necklace indicating the problem. Even though there are a number of organizations providing this type of service, the largest remains the Medic Alert Foundation International. In addition to providing the distinctive metal disk and a wallet card, there is an around-the-clock telephone answering service for access to the member's medical file.

There are a broad array of travel programs tailored to senior citizens. One resource is the American Association of Retired Persons (AARP) which has its own travel service. In addition, many travel agencies cater to the senior traveler, and your local travel agent can provide additional details.

Even though your family physician is an important resource for the international traveler, there are other sources through which you can obtain specific travel medicine information. The U.S. Centers for Disease Control and Prevention (CDC) in Atlanta maintain a telephone travel medicine hotline as well as a travel medicine faxline service that are available to the public. Their phone numbers are:

Travel Medicine Hotline	(404) 332-4559
Travel Medicine Faxline	(404) 332-4565

Internet-savvy people know there is a wealth of travel information available through this medium. Many web sites specifically address travel medicine issues, and a listing of some of these sites is in the accompanying table. You can use various internet "search engines", such as Yahoo and Infoseek, to locate additional travel medicine sites and identify others which address specific medical conditions, unique travel risks, and individual health issues.

TABLE

Internet Travel Medicine Web Sites

- CDC Travel Information:
  http://www.cdc.gov/travel/travel.html

- State Dept Advisories, Travel Warnings, and Consular Information Sheets:
  http://travel.state.gov/travel_warnings.html

- Medical College of Wisconsin International Travelers Clinic:
  http://www.intmed.mcw.edu/travel.html

- The Virtual Hospital: Emporiatrics - An Introduction to Travel Medicine:
  http://indy.radiology.uiowa.edu/Providers/Textbooks/TravelMedicine/TravelMedHP.html

- High Altitude Illness
  http://www.princeton.edu/~rcurtis/altitude.html

- World Health Organization International Travel and Health
  http://jupiter.who.ch/programmes/emc/yellowbook/yb_home.htm

The Medical College of Wisconsin site provides links to a host of www sites, and the WHO site can provide information in multiple languages.

Regardless of the resources contacted, taking the initiative for comprehensive health planning is the traveler's responsibility. Remember, **preventive medicine is not something you get, but rather something you do!**

Health Insurance

As a rule, Blue Cross and Blue Shield are valid internationally but overseas hospitals and physicians will not bill "the Blues" directly. Instead, you'll have to pay the bills personally and then seek reimbursement upon return, remembering this will take several weeks, if not longer. To facilitate repayment, be sure that receipts and records are complete, legible, dated, itemized, and understandable. Preferably, they should be in English. Medical procedures and "treatments" that are considered experimental or investigational, as well as those which are not available in the United States, will not be covered.

Whether insured through Blue Cross/Blue Shield or another private insurer, coverages and limits applicable abroad generally reflect the same services, limitations, and deductibles as those provided domestically. It is important to note, however, that **Medicare and Medicaid coverage does not apply outside the U.S.** The only exception involves urgent medical problems and emergencies arising within Canada when Americans can document that they are traveling between the continental U.S. and Alaska.

If it's been a while since you reviewed your health (and life) insurance coverages, preparing for a trip abroad is the time to do so. Look over your policies, ascertain any limitations and restrictions, and determine whether you need or want supplemental coverage. At the same time, review the procedures that will need to be followed in the unfortunate event that it becomes necessary to file a claim.

The high cost of medical care is not unique to this country and, with standard health insurance coverage, international travelers are entirely on their own abroad. In the face of a serious injury or illness, many thousands of dollars may be needed on the spot. Medical evacuation (needing to be transported from one location to another for medical reasons) could cost thousands more. In most instances, up front cash, credit card payment, or some form of payment guarantee, may be demanded prior to receiving medical care. As a result, more and more travelers are buying supplemental health insurance coverage for protection abroad. There are numerous firms marketing a variety of different type policies. A typical supplemental policy might provide the following types of services:

• Air evacuation, when deemed medically necessary, to either an overseas medical center or else to home. This might be on a commercial, private, or air ambulance type aircraft.
• Referral to a medical care provider overseas, including coverage for expenses incurred for being transported by ambulance, relaying of medical information from home, and communication of important information to relatives at home. Some companies operate toll free hot-lines, 24 hours a day.
• Interest-free loans for paying health care costs or some element of health insurance that provides direct payment of hospital and physician bills.
• Free legal assistance.
• Passport-size medical history forms, occasionally at an additional cost.
• Assistance in the event of a death.

When comparing a number of different supplemental health and accident insurance policies, watch for the following coverages and benefits: help with locating medical care; guarantee of the deposit that hospitals may demand prior to admission; payment of the hospital bill when it is due; and, when adequate treatment facilities are not at hand, evacuation to a center where needed care can be provided.

Many insurance companies try to provide these services in a flexible, convenient and comprehensive manner. Sentry Insurance and the Travelers, for example, have plans that are marketed through many travel agents. Healthcare Abroad has a program which includes basic and major medical benefits, medical evacuation, a provider directory, evidence of insurance that is usually accepted instead of cash for medical services and a 24-hour hotline. There are other companies that provide similar type of services, several are listed in the Appendix.

Health Assessment for Returning Travelers

Global travel has become easier - logistically and politically. Liberal international health regulations have replaced harsh quarantine measures and, as a result, fear of disease has largely disappeared from the international traveler's consciousness. Yet, as alluded to earlier, several recent studies show that a surprisingly large number of U.S. citizens become ill, both while abroad and after returning home. The spectrum of such conditions can be quite diverse, very few are governed by international health regulations and, with the speed of travel today, it is common for many of these diseases not to become apparent until well after the person returns home from a high risk location. **It is therefore vital to tell your doctor where you have been should illness strike after you've been abroad.**

Some high-risk travelers may need to be assessed in a specialized tropical disease/travel medicine clinic upon returning home. Situations which might necessitate travelers availing themselves of such a specialized center include the following:

- Expatriates who lived in tropical regions or developing countries for two or more years
- Travelers who spent extensive periods visiting rural areas away from the usual tourist routes
- Overseas workers who have been in frequent contact with native population groups in developing areas
- Visitors to tropical regions, even for relatively short intervals, who develop symptoms within six months of returning from abroad.

With regard to the latter, examples of symptoms warranting specialized assessment include: high fevers; persistent diarrhea; protracted or recurrent itchy rashes; and an asthma-like cough.

The vast majority of returning travelers, however, will return to the care of their personal physician who will be quite capable of completing any necessary return assessment. As part of a routine return evaluation, the following may be performed depending on the nature and duration of your travel:

- A repeat health assessment (medical history; physical examination—with emphasis on swollen lymph nodes, rashes, insect bites, and enlarged abdominal organs)
- A repeat TB skin test
- A stool examination for helminth eggs and protozoal parasites
- Certain other laboratory tests, including a complete blood count, and possibly a blood smear for malaria parasites

If something suspicious turns up, some of these tests may need to be repeated over the next 7-10 days. Recurrent diarrhea warrants stool cultures in addition to the assessment for ova and parasites, and if persistent, a more aggressive work-up is warranted. If exposure to sexually transmitted disease has been a possibility, this requires evaluation, regardless of the presence or absence of symptoms. **The possibility of latent malaria should be entertained with any febrile illness occurring up to a year after return from a malarious region, even if prophylactic medication was faithfully taken while abroad.**

Chapter Two

Advice On Specific Health Concerns

Heart Disease

Even though there may be some restrictions concerning activities and destinations, people with stable heart conditions (for at least six months) should be able to travel without undue difficulty or risk. Ideally, cardiac patients should be active and with minimal symptoms to get the most out of travel. An exercise tolerance (stress) test before departure might be indicated, and the results reassuring to all concerned. Regardless, travel should reflect the pace and schedule you are accustomed to when at home.

If you have a heart condition, talk to your doctor about whether supplemental oxygen should be used during flight. If so, you'll need to make arrangements with the airline's medical department at least 48 hours before your flight. Because of the rigors of travel, along with the decreased oxygen concentration in the cabin air of a pressurized aircraft, the need for nitroglycerin might exist, and a fresh supply should be taken by all heart patients, even if they had not been using it regularly or recently at home. The medication should be kept conveniently at hand and not stowed away in the checked luggage. If on a low salt, low cholesterol, or other prescribed diet, make arrangements ahead of time with the air carrier or tour director to assure appropriate food is available.

Many cardiac patients have an implanted pacemaker as a part of their therapeutic regimen. If you do, you should be thoroughly evaluated by your cardiologist to ascertain that there is no evidence of pacemaker malfunction prior to going abroad, and make sure there is sufficient battery life remaining in the pulse generator before undertaking any extensive trip. The magnetometers used at airports for security purposes will not adversely affect an implanted pacemaker. Descriptive information about the pacemaker as well as a copy of the EKG tracing should be carried while traveling. Many pacemaker patients are accustomed to having their units checked by electronic telephone diagnostic programs. Unfortunately, these type of calls may not be able to be relayed internationally.

Some heart patients make the decision to travel for rest and relaxation as part of therapy after a heart attack or cardiac surgery. After an uncomplicated heart attack, four to six weeks are customarily allowed to pass before a patient is considered a candidate for a plane trip. Even though it is generally recommended that individuals wait at least two to three weeks after a surgical procedure before flying, longer periods are often required following a major heart operation, and a four to six week delay seems reasonable here, too, assuming the procedure was uncomplicated. In either case, the presence of any complication or instability would influence the decision to travel. Heart failure would make any trip more precarious as would uncontrolled blood pressure problems, unstable cardiac arrhythmias, and the persistence or return of heart pain (angina).

For many cardiac patients with recent symptoms or procedures, a vigorous tour rather than a relaxing vacation requires a more extended deferment, and a delay of at least six months might be more appropriate. If a tour is subsequently considered, pick one that is relaxing rather than hectic, and allow extra time in scheduling, particularly in making connections. Take advantage of curbside luggage check-in and airport transportation systems which minimize exertion. Finally, schedule your tour during a season when extremes of temperature can be avoided, both excessive heat and cold will add to the stress of the trip.

High Blood Pressure

High blood pressure, or hypertension as it is known medically, is an extremely common problem; there are in excess of 34 million adults in the United States with the condition. The diagnosis of hypertension in and of itself does not preclude international travel; however, as with any chronic medical condition, the problem should be adequately controlled and stable on a well tolerated treatment program for a period of at least six months before going overseas. Your family physician can individualize appropriate limitations and precautions. It is important to pack an ample and fresh supply of medications, being certain that what is stowed for the trip represents what is currently prescribed. Important medications should always be placed in the carry-on luggage.

Many patients with high blood pressure take potassium supplementation as a part of their therapy. Sometimes this medication is in liquid form. When traveling, liquid medications are a nuisance to pack because of their bulkiness and the risk of leakage. A powder and effervescent tablet formulation of potassium as well as slow release tablets are available and are more convenient when traveling.

Travel to hot climates, particularly when the change is dramatic, such as winter trips to the tropics, can exaggerate some of the side effects occasionally experienced with antihypertensive medication. The dizziness occasionally encountered with the use of diuretics (fluid pills) can increase but the duration of this discomforting symptom is usually quite brief. It is a normal response for the body to conserve water when visiting a hot region, as part of the adaptation process, and this can cause mild edema (swelling) and occasionally even a slight rise in the blood pressure.

The best management for this includes increased periods of rest, liberal use of air conditioned facilities, and gradual but progressive participation in outdoor activities, avoiding the hottest part of the day. It is advisable to maintain the standard medical regimen during this adjustment phase, with the possible exception of boosting the potassium supplementation, particularly if a digitalis product such as digoxin is taken in addition to a diuretic agent. Do not take salt tablets as is occasionally done in hot climates, but do strive to maintain an adequate fluid intake. Dietary manipulation, the backbone of blood pressure management, is important to continue while traveling. It is easy to consume too much salt while on the road. As has already been mentioned, with sufficient notice, airlines and tour directors can arrange for special diets.

Circulatory Insufficiency

Hippocrates, in the fifth century B.C., first described venous insufficiency of the lower extremities, with observations regarding complications and insights relating to therapy. In the close to 2,500 years that have elapsed since that time, circulatory impairment of the legs continues to plague patients and challenge the medical profession. Problems range from the relatively common nuisance of varicose veins to the more serious inflammatory and ulcerative conditions which at times can be life-threatening.

For individuals with compromised circulation to the lower extremities, travel can be undertaken if certain precautions are followed. For example, prolonged periods of immobilization must be avoided, particularly while flying or during other sedentary travel. Complete immobility can be prevented by occasionally strolling about the plane cabin; and while seated, calf exercises can be performed to stimulate the circulation. Once abroad, similar precautions should be continued. If touring by automobile, stop every hour or two for a brief walk. Wearing elastic support hose can provide comfort and prevent progression of the circulatory insufficiency.

Patients with cerebral insufficiency because of impaired blood flow to the brain often do poorly during flight. Confusion on the ground can only be expected to worsen in the air. If such individuals must travel, there should definitely be an escort. Stroke patients should wait an absolute minimum of three to four weeks before flying. Recovery from the neurologic deficit of a stroke can be exceedingly slow, and it is not uncommon for a set-back in the recovery process to occur as a result of the stress and hypoxia associated with a premature plane trip.

If you are taking blood thinning medication (anticoagulants), extensive travel should be considered only if the degree of anticoagulation is within the therapeutic range, has consistently been so for at least six months, and your medication is being tolerated with no adverse side-effects. A blood test should be done before departure to document the level of treatment and, in addition to wearing the appropriate medical alert identification, you should carry a synopsis of your medical condition and treatment plan. Ideally, you should know the name of a physician or clinic in the locations you're visiting so that they could be contacted if a real or suspected problem develops.

It is important to avoid activities which might increase the probability of serious injury, particularly head trauma and falls when taking anticoagulants. Also, it would be advisable to adhere to a travel itinerary which does not deviate too far off the beaten track. By striving to stay in larger cities and towns overseas, there is some level of assurance that medical care would be more readily available should it be needed.

Pulmonary Disease

Many of the caveats already outlined for patients with underlying cardiac disease are appropriate for those with chronic pulmonary disease as well. Of particular importance is the stability of the respiratory condition and the necessity of tailoring the pace of your activities. A pertinent issue, again, concerns the appropriateness of supplemental oxygen during air travel, and this should be discussed with your physician, who in turn may wish to review the situation with the medical director of the airline. Even though the slight reduction in cabin oxygen concentration is well tolerated by flyers with normal respiratory function, serious difficulty may be experienced by those with chronic breathing disorders who are just borderline compensated. For those familiar with the results of pulmonary testing, extensive traveling and flying should be avoided by those with a vital capacity less than 50% and an arterial oxygen (pO2) determination less than 50 mm Hg.

If oxygen is indicated, it will need to be supplied by the airline. U.S. carriers will not allow the use of personal oxygen while airborne. Transportation of personal canisters is permissible if they are shipped empty as baggage. With 48 hours advance notice, airlines can provide oxygen. The carrier will need instructions from your physician specifying the flow rate and whether oxygen delivery should be continuous or intermittent. Oxygen is usually administered at a rate of 2 to 4 liters/minute (25-30%). A fee of approximately $50-75 per tank for each segment of flight is a customary charge. To reduce the cost of oxygen as well as the stress of making connections, it is best to book direct flights whenever possible rather than to make connections at a hub. At a flow rate of 2 liters/minute, a tank will last approximately 4 hours, and at 4 liters/minute, 2 hours. Airlines will not supply oxygen during layovers, and for that, it will be necessary to contact an oxygen supply company in the layover city. Twenty-fours notice is required, and the oxygen tank will be delivered to the gate.

Some individuals with near normal respiratory function at rest will develop breathing difficulty during the stress of travel. For select patients with chronic lung disease, a stress test prior to the rigors of travel may provide useful information. Recently, an altitude stress test has been introduced during which a patient breathes a gas mixture comparable to the air found at a certain altitude. It may be the altitude of the destination to be visited, or that of the cabin pressure of the aircraft during flight. This test may be helpful in predicting oxygen needs during travel, but unfortunately it is not widely available at the present time.

Flying is complicated by the presence of a respiratory tract infection, and in patients with underlying pulmonary disease, flying is definitely inadvisable during a bronchial infection. It is important to drink sufficient fluids during the flight since the dry cabin air (relative humidity 5-10%) can not only irritate the air passageways, but will make respiratory secretions thicker and more difficult to clear, a situation best avoided by the patient with chronic pulmonary disease. Also, avoid overeating, alcoholic beverages, and sedative medication since all can adversely affect respiratory function, and the latter two can further dry secretions. For those prone to lower respiratory tract infections, discuss with your physician the potential merit of traveling with a supply of an antibiotic medication in the event of need. Certain antibiotics, particularly those that have only recently been approved, may not be universally available.

It goes without saying that pulmonary patients should not smoke, and this is certainly true before, during, and between flights. On selected international flights where smoking is still permitted, every effort should be made to sit in the non-smoking section, at least several rows from the smoking section to avoid the passive inhalation of tobacco smoke. Make use of airline seating priority arrangements, including pre-boarding, and choose a seat strategically located on the aisle and near a lavatory so as to avoid excessive activity during flight. Remember, walking in an aircraft while underway may very well prove to be much more taxing because of the reduced oxygen.

Precautions don't end at the conclusion of the flight. The pace and tempo of activities should continue to reflect the customary pattern of those pursued at home. Medications used and precautions taken at home should be continued. Be particularly cautious of environmental hazards (smog and air pollution are universal problems) and, as much as possible, avoid large metropolitan areas during hours of heavy traffic congestion. There are special filtration masks that minimize exposure to particulate pollution and pollen.

Diabetes

Long distance travel has the potential for affecting diabetic control in a number of ways and some precautions should be exercised. The disruption to daily routines, including activity level and meal consumption, can adversely affect control, as can heightened stress and jet lag.

It is important to discuss travel plans with your physician and specifically ask for guidelines regarding diet, exercise, rest, and possible medication adjustments. For example, the crossing of many time zones in a jet aircraft can lengthen or shorten the day depending on direction of flight, and this can lead to modifications in insulin dosage becoming necessary. The appended table summarizes what is often recommended, but these adjustments are only general guidelines which should be tailored to your particular condition and circumstances.

No drug adjustments are necessary when crossing five or fewer time zones, when flying north and south, or if taking an oral diabetes medication. Be aware that diabetics may be more prone to tissue injury during flight if the blood glucose falls too low, so it is better to keep the level somewhat on the high side during travel than to aggressively strive for absolute control.

Concern about your diet is also important. Airlines and other carriers can provide diabetic diets, when given sufficient advance notice (48 hours). Many diabetic travelers find it prudent to remain on home time throughout the course of the journey as far as meals and medications are concerned (to the fullest extent possible), and then to adjust the schedule of both after arriving at their final destination.

If you're prone to motion sickness, it is important to take medication to prevent it. Protracted episodes of motion sickness can readily precipitate not only the loss of diabetic control, but the development of undesirable and potentially serious complications such as ketoacidosis, a life-threatening complication of diabetes.

During transit, be certain to keep the insulin and related accessories in the carry-on luggage. Insulin should be stored in a cool place, preferably a refrigerator, however, while traveling, the bottle of insulin currently being used may be kept unrefrigerated as long as it is kept as cool as possible and away from heat and direct sunlight. Do not let insulin freeze and do not use any bottle that changes in color or consistency, or which has expired. Insulin can be obtained without difficulty, in most overseas locations, but care must be exercised to purchase the same strength as the accustomed variety.

It is a wise precaution for diabetics to carry one or two candy bars with them at all times while traveling, since altered schedules and activity levels may subject them to hypoglycemic reactions. In warm environments where it may be impractical to carry candy, small plastic squeeze bottles filled with a commercially available glucose concentrate are a popular and feasible alternative. It is wise to be familiar with the symptoms of a hypoglycemic (low blood sugar) reaction, and to know what should be done immediately to combat such a situation. Some diabetics have been instructed to carry and administer glucagon to pharmacologically treat impending hypoglycemia. **Diabetics are strongly urged to wear a medic alert identification tag at all times, particularly when traveling, and to carry additional information which details the insulin dose and regimen.**

Since travel can be hard on the feet, and diabetics are prone to foot problems, this is another area for extra precaution. In addition to using discretion regarding the nature and amount of activities planned, be sure to wear comfortable shoes that are broken-in before departure. By following the precautions described and the advice of one's personal physician, there is no reason why most diabetics shouldn't be able to travel with safety and comfort.

TABLE

*Insulin Adjustment During Jet Travel Across Multiple Time Zones**

EASTBOUND

DAILY INSULIN REGIMEN	DAY OF DEPARTURE	1ST MORNING AT DESTINATION	10 HOURS AFTER AM DOSE	2ND DAY AT DESTINATION
Single Dose Schedule	Usual Dose	2/3 Usual Dose	Remaining 1/3 AM Dose if Blood Sugar (BS) Over 240	Usual Dose
Two Dose Schedule	Usual AM & Evening Doses	2/3 Usual Morning Dose	Usual evening Dose & Remaining 1/3 AM Dose if BS over 240	Usual Two Doses

WESTBOUND

DAILY INSULIN REGIMEN	DAY OF DEPARTURE	18 HOURS AFTER AM DOSE	FIRST DAY AT DESTINATION
Single Dose Schedule	Usual Dose	1/3 Usual Dose Followed by Snack if BS Over 240	Usual Dose
Two Dose Schedule	Usual AM & Evening Doses	1/3 Usual AM Dose Followed by Snack if BS over 240	Usual Two Doses

*Adapted from Benson and Metz: "Management of Diabetes during Intercontinental Travel," Bull Mason Clinic, 38:145-151, Winter 1984-5; and Jong EC: "The Travel and Tropical Medicine Manual," W. B. Saunders and Co., Philadelphia, 1987.

Arthritis

Many people consider some arthritis a normal part of the aging process, although the severity and symptoms can vary widely. Unfortunately, travel can aggravate symptoms, even when the condition had been relatively stable. The reasons include the change in pace, generally increased activity, the temptation to carry more than is prudent, the propensity for prolonged periods of sitting enroute as well as standing after arrival, and the necessity to accommodate to strange sleeping arrangements and unfamiliar activities.

When arduous travel is contemplated, important preparation goes beyond packing the aspirin and liniment, though both can be important. Attaining and maintaining a better level of conditioning can go a long way to alleviate symptoms, particularly chronic back pain. Before departing on any long trip, a regular regimen of stretching exercises, modified endurance training, and physical conditioning is an important part of a rehabilitation and prevention program. If not usually done, exercise should become part of everyday activities for at least 2-3 weeks before an extensive trip. The regimen should be continued once underway. Since traveling is often characterized by endless hours of sitting, a routine that includes a morning walk, a conscientious attempt to use stairs rather than the elevator, and a regularly designated interval for stretching exercises can be very helpful.

Also beneficial in controlling back pain is learning how to relax and specific relaxation techniques are important skills to learn. The combination of exercise and relaxation, in conjunction with specific individualized precautions prescribed by your family physician, can help prevent this frequent and chronic complaint from jeopardizing daily activities, be it travel or otherwise.

When sitting for long durations, a pillow or rolled-up blanket against the lower back can produce symptomatic relief. When traveling by plane, request an aisle seat. This allows you to stretch and have unhampered access to the aisle. Use care in packing, take 2-3 small suitcases instead of one large one and use the type that have built-in wheels and pull-straps. Be easy on yourself, use porters, luggage carts, and airport conveyance systems when available and appropriate. Be careful when you must lift heavy luggage - test it first and employ correct lifting techniques, using leg muscles rather than those of your arms and back.

Nervous Conditions

Headaches are a common problem, one of the most frequent causes of visits to a physician and absences from school and work. Headaches can also be common during travel, even for those who do not customarily experience them. For frequent head pain sufferers, travel can be a real challenge. Migraines are thought to affect upwards of 19% of women and 6% of men, and many activities and changes associated with international travel can be a migraine trigger. These not only include changes in activity, dietary, and sleep patterns; climatic and altitude fluctuations; but also physical and emotional stress, jet lag, travel fatigue, and the very act of flying in a pressurized aircraft. Many of these triggers can be difficult to control, so appropriate anti-headache medications should be kept accessible, being careful not to provoke analgesic rebound headaches by overusing pain and decongestant medications. People who get frequent migraines should discuss with their physician possible modifications to their daily maintenance medications before extensive travel.

Travel often invokes anxiety even in otherwise psychologically stable individuals. Those prone to panic attacks, as well as those who are unstable from a psychological standpoint, often have more intense problems while traveling for a number of reasons, including sleep deprivation, jet lag, travel fatigue, unusual and varied sensory stimuli, frequent and close proximity to strangers, recurrent changes in schedule and location, as well as unexpected delays. If you are still in, or recently discharged from therapy, you should review travel plans with your therapist. The motivating reason(s) for traveling abroad are important in predicting trip related recurrences of psychological and emotional difficulties.

For all travelers, it is helpful to understand the motivation for contemplating a long trip, particularly one planned spontaneously. To pursue an arduous, challenging, adventure packed trip for the challenge of it, the "because it's there" attitude, presents no major difficulty as long as one can accept set-backs and disappointment. Certainly global travel is not the arena for instant gratification. Many travelers pursue this activity for the enjoyment, education, and the more contained adventure and excitement it affords. Here there is rarely any disappointment. However, there are a few who venture solely as an escape mechanism, a futile search for Utopia. This running from a problem or searching for the "geographic cure" is much more likely to result in disappointment, disillusionment and depression. More will be said about psychological stressors, defense mechanisms, and adjustment processes in the section on retirement abroad.

Travelers with a recent or unstable psychiatric history who must travel should do so with an escort, preferably someone well known to them who has the skill and expertise to handle the situation should a crisis arise. Sedation prior to departure may be of benefit: however care must be taken in choosing the drug since some medications can produce undesirable consequences, including agitation, when flying. In the past, Halcion (triazolam) was often prescribed for rest and sleep during travel, and unfortunately this product led to the development of serious memory problems in many users. The condition became referred to as "travelers' amnesia," and older travelers were at enhanced risk, particularly if the medication was taken in conjunction with an alcoholic beverage.

Sometimes the excitement and anxiety of air travel can result in hyperventilation, a reaction caused by breathing too fast. Symptons can include tingling in the lips and fingers and sometimes more frightening reactions including shortness of breath and chest pains. If this should occur, it can be relieved by breathing into a paper bag (such as an air sickness bag), a handbag, or any small container that is readily available.

Anticipating psychological problems that may occur while traveling is an important part of preparing for your trip. Frightful experiences aren't quite so harrowing when they are understood rather than occuring mysteriously and unexpectedly.

The Handicapped Traveler

In recent years, there have been a number of developments which greatly benefit handicapped individuals who want to enjoy global travel. The majority of these actually pre-date passage of The Americans with Disabilities Act. Because of this heightened level of consciousness regarding the obstacles faced by physically challenged citizens, there has been a movement towards the removal of barriers - both physical and social

— along with other technological advances. A number of resources have also been developed to assist the handicapped traveler, either in providing pertinent information or in operating tours specifically for the disabled.

Even though travel for the handicapped may not yet be easy or affordable, it is feasible. Considerable credit for that goes to an organization with which all disabled travelers should be familiar, The Society for the Advancement of Travel for the Handicapped (SATH). This organization holds frequent seminars and publishes a free newsletter that is sent to members. The Travel Information Center at the Moss Rehabilitation Hospital provides general information on travel opportunities for the disabled and will answer individual questions.

There are a number of tour companies which specialize in arranging trips for the handicapped, a few of which are listed in the Appendix. Most travel agents can provide additional information. The following is some general information that the disabled traveler should know.

• Airlines and aircraft manufacturers have instituted changes that help the wheelchaired traveler. For example, most aircraft are able to accommodate an aisle chair (a small wheelchair) and have movable arm rests to facilitate transfer. In addition, some have modified restroom facilities to accommodate the wheelchaired traveler. Air carriers should be able to provide wheelchair availability, rapid transportation within the terminal, pre-boarding priority, preferred seat selection, lifts in the absence of jetways, and free transportation of a personal wheelchair. When flying, handicapped travelers should specify seating requirements in advance, advising the carrier that they use a wheelchair when making reservations, indicating whether or not an attendant will be escorting them on the trip, and arriving at the terminal at least one hour prior to departure.

• For the vision and hearing impaired, provisions abroad have not kept pace with accommodations domestically. Guide dogs for the visually impaired do not receive the same latitude overseas as they do in the U.S., and in some areas may actually be subject to long-term quarantine. The animals may be forbidden in certain overseas establishments and onboard foreign transportation carriers. The hearing impaired may experience a relative absence of TTY services and amplified telephones. Unfortunately, both vision and hearing impaired travelers may find an absence of ways to relay important emergency information.

Chapter Three

Disease Prevention

Basic Immunization

The topic of adult immunization is in vogue these days. In the past, immunization policies were primarily directed toward protecting infants, children and adolescents, but this is no longer the case. The subject of adult immunization can be considered in several different reference frames, including age groups, special occupations, lifestyles, environmental situations, and international travel itineraries.

In regard to recommendations that universally apply, all adults should be current with their diphtheria and tetanus booster shots, and senior citizens should avail themselves of influenza and pneumococcal pneumonia vaccine protection.

Diphtheria and Tetanus

Diphtheria is an acute bacterial infection characterized by the development of a membrane in the throat and the production of a toxin by the responsible germ which damages the heart muscle and nervous system. The disease has a worldwide distribution but is more common in temperate climates than in the tropics. It is prevalent in most developing countries where crowding, improper hygiene, and inadequate immunization prevail.

Adults are at risk if unvaccinated, but the risk of international travelers contracting diphtheria while abroad is thought to be quite low. However, when it became apparent that a disproportionate portion of domestic cases were occurring in adults over the age of 50, and that over 80% of adults beyond the age of 60 were susceptible to this disease, it became standard practice to provide a booster dose of diphtheria toxoid every ten years in conjunction with tetanus.

Tetanus (lockjaw) is a serious disease of the nervous system caused by a potent toxin which is produced by the infecting bacteria. In a typical case, spores of this germ, often after lying dormant in the soil, contaminate a puncture-type wound. The responsible microbe appears to be ubiquitous in the environment; the disease is most commonly encountered in warmer, overcrowded, highly cultivated, and economically deprived regions where there are inadequate vaccination practices.

Over half the U.S. cases occur in adults over the age of 60, and 2/3 of Americans past the age of 60 have inadequate protection. The risk does not appear to be increased with global travel. However, because so many older Americans are susceptible to diphtheria and tetanus, principally because it has been so long since a booster shot was administered, an overseas trip is an opportune occasion for updating this inoculation. A combination tetanus diphtheria (Td) booster should be administered every 10 years, and a booster every mid decade birthday (35, 45, 55, etc.) is a helpful way to remember. If it has been more than five years since the last booster was administered, it is a good idea to get a pre-departure Td booster shot. Not only will this assure that protection is in place, it will avoid the need for getting a booster overseas if an injury should be sustained.

Influenza

International travel, per se, is not a reason for getting a flu shot. However, individuals for whom this annual immunization is recommended should make it a point of getting vaccinated before departing on a winter vacation. Since 1963, the CDC has issued annual recommendations regarding protection against influenza, and rather consistently, only about 20% of those at increased risk have heeded this advice. Consequently, it is not uncommon to record an extra 10,000 deaths annually in the U.S. related to the consequences of this disease.

Influenza is a viral disease of the lower respiratory tract causing cough, fever, and other complaints. Complications include primary influenza (viral) pneumonia and secondary bacterial pneumonia, both of which frequently strike individuals who, because of their age or underlying health status, are poorly able to cope with this illness.

Flu vaccine should be administered in the autumn before cases of the disease begin to get reported. Most recommend that it be received by mid November, remembering that it takes several weeks for protection to occur following the inoculation. Since protection tends to wane with time, getting the shot too early in the fall runs the risk of having inadequate protection should influenza not show up until late February or March. Getting the shot much after Thanksgiving runs the risk of flu occurring in the community before an appropriate antibody response has occurred following vaccination.

Pneumococcal Pneumonia

Candidates for an annual flu shot may very well be candidates for pneumococcal vaccine as well. This vaccine, which provides protection against a common variety of bacterial pneumonia, is administered on a one time only basis rather than annually. It is indicated for those with a variety of medical conditions, and in addition, it should be given to all at age 65.

VACCINES THAT MAY BE REQUIRED

Yellow Fever

Yellow fever, a viral illness transmitted by the Aedes aegypti mosquito, is a disease for which immunization may be required for international travel. The disease is regularly reported in equatorial Africa as well as in parts of South America, primarily in regions between 15 degrees north and 15 degrees south latitude. Because of inaccuracies in diagnosis and inconsistencies in reporting, it is difficult to be certain which countries or areas within endemic regions represent the greatest threat. In the Western Hemisphere, yellow fever occasionally extends into Central America and the Caribbean, nevertheless it is regarded as being a rare illness among international travelers.

Yellow fever can be prevented with a single injection of a live virus vaccine. This protection is thought to be present within ten days of inoculation and to last for approximately ten years. Yellow fever vaccines must be approved by the World Health Organization and administered at approved vaccination centers. State and local health departments can refer international travelers to the closest vaccination center and can confirm the necessity for obtaining this particular inoculation. It is recommended that travelers get vaccinated against yellow fever if they will be going to or passing through any country in which the disease is reported.

This vaccine is prepared in tissue culture, being grown in chick embryos, so those allergic to eggs theoretically may experience a hypersensitivity reaction after vaccination. If at low risk for yellow fever, you should request a letter of waiver from your doctor which clearly states the reasons why the vaccine should not be administered. This statement should be on letterhead stationery and taken to a designated yellow fever immunization center where it should be stamped with the center's official seal. Since this may not be accepted by all governments, it is a good idea to contact the local embassies or consulates of the countries to be visited to obtain authoritative advice and a letter substantiating the waiver of requirements.

People with a documented allergic reaction of a severe nature to eggs and who are also at high risk of exposure of yellow fever infection can be skin tested to document allergy to the vaccine. Those at high risk of both allergy and infection should modify their travel plans. For the majority of international travelers, however, yellow fever vaccination will represent a minor inconvenience producing safe and long lasting protection.

Cholera

The situation regarding cholera vaccine continues to be in a state of flux. Both the World Health Organization and the CDC have reported that no country requires cholera vaccination for arriving travelers. Nevertheless, it is known that local authorities in some developing countries still "unofficially" require cholera vaccine as a condition of entry. In such circumstances the arriving visitor is in a difficult situation: either at risk of being immunized on the spot with a questionable product using injection equipment of uncertain cleanliness, or being denied entry, with the potential for total disruption of the travel itinerary.

Consequently, there may still be a need or "requirement" for this vaccine. Certainly cholera is a public health threat in developing countries around the world. Contamination of food and water with infected excrement plays a major role in transmission. Raw and inadequately cooked seafood harvested from sewage-polluted waters are particularly important sources of infection. Consequently, preventive strategies rely much more on food and water precautions, as will be discussed later, than they do on immunization practices.

Cases of cholera among international travelers are considered to be extremely rare. The currently available vaccine is of very limited usefulness, affording only minimal protection against older strains of the cholera bacteria, and none against currently circulating strains. It is interesting to note that in one study of cholera occurring in international travelers (there were only 10 cases in over a decade of surveillance), 80% of the cases occurred in individuals who had been vaccinated! A new oral vaccine has been developed, and approval for use in the U.S. is forthcoming. At the time of this writing, however, it is still not available.

In regard to the currently employed injectable vaccine, a single dose is sufficient to meet international health requirements, and a certificate of such vaccination is valid for a period of six months. In order to avoid the border-crossing hassles and risks mentioned above, certain international travelers should have their International Certificate of Vaccination stamped that they received this inoculation. This would include those travelers who will be visiting several developing countries and crossing borders in which one of the countries being visited is listed as a cholera-infected country. Otherwise, this inoculation is generally not recommended.

Nevertheless, because of the low level of protection this product does afford, there are some individuals who are not only candidates for vaccination, but who should get the complete primary series of inoculations (two injections a month apart). This would include travelers who will be going abroad to work and live in a developing region under less than adequate sanitary conditions for a prolonged period of time, particularly if they will be without prompt access to medical care. It also includes some individuals with predisposing medical conditions, notably those with impaired gastric defense mechanisms. The responsible bacteria is quite sensitive to gastric (stomach) acid, and in a healthy traveler, a small amount of ingested bacteria would likely be inactivated in the stomach. Consequently, individuals with altered gastric defense mechanisms have a somewhat enhanced risk of contracting this disease. Such travelers include those on intense antacid or other ulcer therapy, those with previous gastrectomy surgery for peptic ulcer disease, and those with an inherent inability to produce stomach acid (achlorhydria). Regardless, the best defense against cholera is to avoid food and water which may be contaminated.

VACCINES THAT MAY BE RECOMMENDED

There are many vaccines that on occasion may be recommended, either because of local disease patterns within the places to be visited, risk factors associated with the activities that are being planned, or the unique health profile of the traveler. A synopsis of some of the recommended vaccines follows.

Hepatitis A

Hepatitis A vaccine is new since the previous edition of this book, having become available in the U.S. in 1995. For the most part it has replaced the use of and need for immune globulin (gamma globulin). Hepatitis A is a viral infection of the liver which was previously referred to as infectious hepatitis. It is prevalent worldwide, and like cholera, is transmitted through the ingestion of contaminated food and water. However, in this case, a real threat to international travelers in known to exist.

The vaccine is indicated for all susceptible travelers to less developed and developing regions of the world, particularly if they make frequent short-term visits or are engaged in longer-term international travel. Many older travelers may be naturally immune to hepatitis A, largely because of mild or even sub-clinical (asymptomatic) infection earlier in life, usually childhood. Consequently, before considering immunization against hepatitis A, it may be prudent to have a blood test performed for hepatitis A immunity (antibodies).

For those at risk, hepatitis A vaccine is recommended, and the vaccine is particularly important for older travelers as the risk of serious infection increases with age, especially for persons age 40 and older. Whereas the overall fatality rate is about 0.3%, it is 2-3% (10 times higher) for reported cases in persons aged 40 years and older. Hepatitis A vaccine is given as a single shot with a booster administered 6-12 months later depending on the product used (there are two approved vaccines). It takes at least 2 weeks for effective immunity to occur. The vaccine is safe and side-effects are few.

For those at risk of hepatitis A who need immediate protection, immune globulin may still be necessary. An injection of immune globulin shortly before departure can provide protection for up to 4-5 months depending on the dose administered. Immune globulin, which is a blood-derived product, can be given in conjunction with hepatitis A vaccine in order to acquire both short and longer term protection.

Typhoid

Typhoid is a bacterial infection of the digestive track that, again is spread by fecal contamination of food and water. Person-to-person spread is often the result of careless food handlers. The disease is characterized by fever, fatigue, headache, abdominal pain, and the development of a dark red splotchy rash of the upper abdomen and lower chest. The infection can be progressive to the point of intestinal bleeding and coma.

The risk of contracting typhoid is considered to be low and is greatest for those visiting countries with warm climates and underdeveloped sanitary systems for sewage treatment and water purification. Once again, food and water precautions constitute the primary preventive strategy. At the present time there is an oral as well as an injectable vaccine, with the former being more effective, better tolerated, and with fewer side-effects. There are some individuals who may be candidates for typhoid vaccine who should not receive the oral product, however, including pregnant women, travelers with an altered immune status, those with an acute gastrointestinal illness, and patients on antibiotic therapy. Typhoid vaccine should be considered if going to a developing country for three weeks or longer, particularly if deviating off the usual tourist routes when visiting smaller villages and rural areas, and if eating local cuisine from less well established vendors.

Rabies

Rabies is a viral infection of the nervous system with the most common mode of transmission being through the bite of a rabid animal. Other methods of transmission are known to exist, but these are less important to the international traveler. Whereas in the U.S. wild animals are the primary risk factor, overseas, because of the lack of animal control and vaccination programs, the principal threat remains the dog. More than half of U.S. rabies cases are diagnosed in returning travelers and immigrants as a result of exposure to dogs outside the country.

The overall risk is low, and is likely highest for children who may be more inclined to approach a stray animal. Following a bite, it is imperative that early treatment be obtained. Once symptoms develop, death almost always occurs. In the history of the world there are only three reported cases of survival. The crux of the problem lies in getting early treatment; in the locations where the risk is greatest, the availability of post-exposure therapy is frequently most onerous.

Prevention lies in taking extra precautions in avoiding strange, stray, and wild animals, particularly dogs. If bitten by an animal while overseas, contact the local health authorities, the closest U.S. embassy or consulate, and if the latter are not available, the CDC in Atlanta:

Normal Business Hours	(404) 639-1075 or 1050
Other Times	(404) 639-2888

There is a pre-exposure vaccine that is administered as a series of three injections. It can be used to protect travelers when exposure risk might be high or inapparent and when post-exposure treatment might be delayed or sub-optimal. The vaccine is generally reserved for travelers who will be visiting a high-risk region for more than 30 days. These locations include most countries in Asia (except Taiwan and Japan), most countries in Africa, as well as most in Latin America. Individuals engaged in certain activities when overseas should also consider pre-exposure protection. These would include hunters, trekkers, cave explorers, researchers, and animal care workers.

Although the currently available vaccines are much better tolerated than the older products, there is still a relatively high frequency of side-effects. Pre-exposure vaccination does not preclude the need for avoiding animals, wound treatment in the event of a bite, or more definitive post-exposure management. It provides some relative degree of protection and decreases the extent of the post-exposure treatment.

Poliomyelitis

Polio (Infantile Paralysis) is another viral infection of the nervous systems. For the older traveler, memories of the horror of polio may still be quite vivid...but things have changed. There have been no cases of person-to-person transmission of polio in the Western Hemisphere for a number or years. The last reported case occurred in Peru in August, 1991. Elsewhere, such as in Africa, Asia, the Middle East, and Eastern Europe, there is still some level of transmission. Whereas about 5,000 cases per year get reported, it is thought that closer to 100,000 cases per year tend to occur.

Current domestic immunization programs call for everyone to receive the complete primary series of polio vaccine and a one-time booster dose. Those not having received the above who will be going to an at-risk region are candidates for a booster dose. It is recommended that the booster be the inactivated injectable (Salk) vaccine rather than the live oral sugar-cube (Sabin) product.

Despite the remarkable strides which have been made in eradicating the disease, polio is still in the headlines, as a change in immunization policy was orchestrated in early 1997. The oral vaccine contains a weak but live virus, and although it is considered to be more effective that the inactivated vaccine, it can, on rare occasions, result in clinical polio. Between 1980 and 1994 there were 133 cases of polio in the U.S., and 125 of these were associated with use of the oral vaccine. Consequently, after 40 years of promoting the live vaccine, there has been a movement back to the inactivated one.

Japanese B Encephalitis

This is another viral infection of the nervous system which is endemic to Asia. The overall risk to travelers is again low, but the available data would suggest that the risk of clinical infection, as well as more severe neurologic symptoms and a fatal outcome, increase with the age of the traveler. The risk for more profound illness is greatest in those over 55 years of age.

A vaccine is available, but it is not indicated for all travelers to Asia. Immunization is usually reserved for those who will be visiting for a month or longer in highly endemic rural (pig farming and rice growing) areas, during the transmission season, which is related to both rainy weather and bird migration patterns. In temperate regions the transmission season is May-September, and in tropical and subtropical regions it is more variable. Tourists, in general, are not considered at high risk and rarely are candidates for this particular vaccine.

Meningococcal Meningitis

Meningococcal meningitis is yet another nervous system infection caused by a virus. It occurs on a sporadic basis worldwide, but large regional epidemics can heighten the risk of transmission to the international traveler. The disease is most common in poor, overcrowded areas, and it manifests some seasonal variability, with increased rates reported during winter and spring. The disease is more common in children, but during epidemics, adults are also at increased risk.

Meningitis torments arid sub-Saharan regions of Africa (the Meningitis Belt) during the dry season (December to June), particularly in the western areas. The World Health Organization has reported an increase in sub-Saharan meningitis activity in recent years. In fact, 1996 was the worst year on record.

Meningitis epidemics also occur somewhat more erratically in other countries and regions, including the Middle East. There is a vaccine against some, but not all strains of the meningococcus, which is sometimes indicated among international travelers. Saudi Arabia is the only country that may require proof of vaccination, and this is required for Umra performers and pilgrims to Mecca for the annual Hajj. The U.S. encourages immunization for everybody arriving is Saudi Arabia during the Hajj period.

Vaccination is also recommended for some travelers who will be visiting certain countries that might be experiencing an epidemic, especially if there will be prolonged or close contact with the local populace. At the present time, this would include travel to sub-Saharan Africa during the dry season, and travel to Burundi, Kenya, Tanzania, Nepal, or New Delhi (India) at any time of the year.

Hepatitis B

Hepatitis B is a viral infection of the liver and differs from hepatitis A in terms of severity, transmissions routes, and outcome. Previously referred to as serum hepatitis, it is a more severe disease than hepatitis A. The virus is found in blood, semen, and a variety of other body fluids. Transmission routes of concern to the international traveler include exposure to blood and blood products; use of contaminated needles, razors, toothbrushes, dental and medical equipment; tattooing and ear piercing devices; and sexual contact. The epidemiology of hepatitis B is similar to that of the human immunodeficiency virus (HIV), the germ that causes AIDS, and more will be said about that in a future section. The hepatitis B virus is much more than HIV, however, having the capacity to survive on inanimate objects and dry surfaces for prolonged periods.

The disease is prevalent worldwide where it is a major cause of acute and chronic hepatitis, cirrhosis of the liver, and primary liver cancer. The regions most affected include China and Southeast Asia, the majority of Africa, most of the Pacific islands, parts of the Middle East, the Amazon Basin, and the island of Hispaniola (Haiti and the Dominican Republic), where 8-15% of local population groups are chronically infected.

There is a safe and effective vaccine which has been incorporated into general immunization practices. It is administered as a three-dose series at 0, 1, and 6 months. For travelers, two accelerated dosing schedules can be implemented:

0, 1, and 4 months
0, 1, 2, and 12 months

Many adults may be susceptible to hepatitis B infection, at risk of exposure, and a candidate for immunization whether traveling or not. In terms of international travel, the following individuals would be candidates for immunization:

• Those going abroad for six months or longer, especially if visiting a region of increased risk, living in a rural area, having daily physical contact with the local populace, or receiving local medical or dental care.
• Those who will be involved in healthcare practices while abroad, or who might be having intimate contact with local residents. (See the table regarding AIDS precautions)

Chapter Four

Problems Specific to Travelers

Fear of Flying

If you're afraid to fly, you're not alone. Although there is little argument that flying is the safest way to travel, reluctance to fly is common and one-sixth of all American adults are afraid to do so. Aviophobia can strike even experienced flyers, and it's estimated that one person in four who does fly will develop this fear to an appreciable extent at some point in their lifetime.

For many travelers, the fear of disaster is the phobia's source. However for some, the greatest concern is either the enclosed claustrophobic sensation experienced in the cabin of the aircraft, or the turbulence that might be encountered during the flight. Despite the concern over the latter, "white-knuckling" it is unjustified, particularly during the cruising phase of the flight, when turbulence is most often experienced, as this happens to be the safest part of the flight pattern.

Fear of flying can be controlled. Relaxation exercises before and during flight can help to keep evolving anxiety under control. Some believe that learning the rudiments of how an aircraft flies and the logistics of how the air traffic control network functions can also be reassuring. Visiting an airport and observing the procession of planes taking off and landing can also be settling. Everyday in the U.S. over 3,000 aircraft fly in excess of 1.5 million travelers an average of

600 miles from more than 400 airports without accident or incident. For every one hour a plane spends in flight it spends many more on the ground being serviced. Finally, there is reassurance in the fact that being an airline pilot is not regarded as being a hazardous occupation by the insurance industry. Unless one flies as a test pilot, life insurance rates are standard.

For those ill-at-ease when the decision is made to fly, schedule a morning flight so you can get going without spending the entire day feeling uneasy. Also, allow plenty of time for getting to the airport, checking in, and clearing security. Rushing exaggerates anxiety.

If you need additional help, specific workshops on the fear of flying are available which are considered quite effective. Many airlines offer programs aimed at controlling this fear. Also, some clinical psychologists offer services designed to help control aviophobia. Contact an airline or travel agent or the resources listed in the Appendix.

Air Travel Precautions

Despite the safety and comfort of modern air travel, there are still some individuals who may not be candidates for this mode of travel. The information on specific health concerns included recommendations regarding precautions on travel in general and air travel in particular. This section further describes certain recommendations and precautions regarding air travel.

Individuals who are physically ill tend to do poorly when flying. If at all possible, those with an acute illness should attempt to defer their travel plans until symptoms remit. Those with a more chronic illness need more careful attention, particularly if their condition is unstable or in its advanced stages. Ideally, chronic conditions should be stable and symptoms reasonably well controlled. Having said that, it is recognized that those seriously and even terminally ill may wish to travel for a variety of reasons, ranging from visiting family members one last time to seeking some sort of medical treatment or intervention. Airlines are aware of this and tend to be accommodating, but they will deny passage to individuals unlikely to survive the journey, those with known contagious or communicable diseases that are a public health concern, and those with extensive skin disease.

Other patients with chronic conditions may be able to fly, but still warrant special consideration. For example, patients with different forms of anemia may be more sensitive to the subtle changes in cabin pressure and oxygen concentration that are encountered while airborne. Current federal regulations specify that an aircraft must be able to maintain an 8,000 foot cabin environment at its highest operating altitude. This can drop the oxygen level in the blood by up to 1/3, and even though this level of hypoxia is generally not detectable by healthy individuals, anemic patients, as well as those with certain sickle cell conditions, are at risk and warrant individual assessment. Sickle cell trait, generally regarded as a benign condition, can lead to sickling crisis at high altitudes and when flying, even in pressurized aircraft.

Many in the convalescent phase of an illness or surgical procedure may desire to travel for rest and convalescence. Nevertheless, it is important to allow sufficient time to pass following a surgical procedure so that the rigours of travel and flying do not complicate the healing process. As an absolute minimum, 10 days should elapse following routine surgery before flying, and for uncomplicated head and chest surgery, the delay should be a minimum of 3 weeks. A week should elapse following any diagnostic procedure in which air was injected into a body cavity, such as during a barium enema. However with pneumoencephalography (which is rarely done anymore), a procedure in which air is injected into the central nervous system, a delay of 2 weeks is advisable.

New fractures, fractures of the lower extremity, and fractures with unsplit casts make flying inadvisable. Fractures of the jaw with fixed wiring preclude flying because of the risk of vomiting and aspiration in the event of motion sickness.

Some dentists recommend that air travel be avoided for three days after a scraping procedure if there is extensive inflammation present. Likewise, air travel should be avoided following a tooth extraction either for three days or for as long as bleeding continues to occur. Air may be trapped deep in the socket near the base where the old root existed and because of expansion of this air during flight, severe pain and resumed bleeding might occur.

Both a recent stroke and heart attack warrant delays as already mentioned. In the face of chronic cardiovascular disease, travel should be deferred if there is persistent chest pain, heart failure, cardiac arrhythmia, or uncontrolled hypertension. For cerebrovascular disease, neurologic symptoms which are evolving or the occurrence of seizures likewise warrant postponement of travel plans.

For patients with chronic lung disease, recommendations regarding limitations and supplemental oxygen were described earlier. Those with a history of emphysema, chronic bronchitis or a history of pneumothorax (collapsed lung) require additional assessment. For some, flying is clearly not indicated. For those with chronic gastrointestinal conditions, acute diverticulitis or colitis, as well as a history of peptic ulcer disease with bleeding, travel should be delayed until symptoms have been inactive for at least three weeks.

Even for the healthy there are safeguards. For example, for those travelers who like to scuba dive, adequate time must elapse between the last dive and flying, otherwise the bends might develop while airborne. Do not dive and fly the same day, but, if no decompression diving is done, it will be safe to fly the following day. If you've done decompression diving or if you're uncertain, wait 36 hours.

Jet Lag

Jet lag is always a fashionable topic for discussion. Even though some mild symptoms of jet lag may show up after crossing only three time zones, it usually takes four or five time zone changes to produce more consistent and dramatic effects. Jet lag is an interruption to one's customary cyclical rhythm, caused by modification to the day-night cycle. Eastward travel in effect shortens the day, whereas westward travel lengthens it. In either case just about all of the body's metabolic systems can be affected and result in altered performance, function, and sleep.

Transmeridian travel in most individuals will produce some impairment to judgment and performance, so it is problematic to attempt to consummate an important business deal or engage in a hectic social schedule too soon after arriving at a distant location. It is common for jet lag to be more noticeable when flying East than when going West. There are a number of reasons for this, one is the fact that in most individuals, natural body rhythms tend to run slightly longer than 24 hours. Another is the happenstance that long westward travel tends to lead to an arrival time close to the bedtime for the local population. On the other hand, eastbound travelers tend to arrive at their destination after a fitful and abbreviated night on a plane in time to see a new day dawn and when the local population is getting up. For example, a traveler departing JFK for Europe at 6:00 p.m. may very well cross seven time zones during a seven hour flight. Arriving in Europe at 8:00 a.m. local time, our beleaguered jet setter feels as if it's 1:00 a.m. and is much more interested in ending rather than beginning the day.

Even though gradually switching one's cycle to the time zone of the intended destination prior to departure works for some travelers, this is difficult for most to accomplish. A better approach, if at all possible, is to schedule a morning flight that will arrive at a time close to the body's accustomed bedtime and to rest on arrival. It is wise to allow one day for rest after crossing four to six time zones, and two days if seven to ten zones are crossed.

After arriving overseas, attempt to schedule the most important activities at a time when energy levels appear to be at their peak. When rescheduling becomes necessary, shorten the day and not the night. This will assist in the gradual resetting of rhythms and not detract from the most valuable recuperative jet lag aid: sleep. Because jet lag at best is a nuisance and inconvenience and at its worse a curse that can undermine the trip, there is a growing interest in minimizing its effects. In recent years a number of approaches have been tried including dietary manipulation, activity modification, pharmaceutical administration, and scheduling variation.

Recently the combination of melatonin administration in conjunction with light therapy has been in vogue. Melatonin, the so-called timekeeping hormone, is the natural chemical which enables the body to adjust to day/night changes. Produced by the pineal gland in the brain, melatonin is naturally released at a rate which is inversely related to environmental lighting. Melatonin is readily available at health food stores and pharmacies without a prescription but there are unanswered questions regarding its safety and efficacy. The evidence, to date, does suggest that melatonin administration, either with or without light therapy, can facilitate jet lag adjustment. The two interventions are complementary as light tends to be a daytime signal and melatonin a nighttime one. The light generally used is the same as that employed for seasonal affective disorder, daylight intensity light, which is approximately five times brighter than ordinary indoor light. The melatonin doses that have been used have been quite varied. Products containing 3 mg (milligrams) are readily available, and this is in all likelihood an ample dose; the body secretes between 5-25 micrograms per day. Before using melatonin, however, check with your physician to be certain that there are no reasons why you should not.

If given the green light, the regimen to be employed depends on the direction of travel, and when used, many travelers try to begin the intervention a couple of days before departure. To shift the body clock earlier, as would be desirable with eastward travel, one could use light therapy in the morning and melatonin in the late afternoon or early evening. For those flying west, one would want to shift the body clock later, and in this situation one could use melatonin in the early morning and light therapy in the late afternoon or early evening. Taking melatonin during the day can result in some sleepiness, and this has lead to use of the product as a "natural" sleeping aid.

Another popular intervention has been the so-called jet lag diet, which consists of alternating feasts and fasts beginning three days before departing on an international trip. The regimen received some publicity when former President Reagan employed it while visiting the Orient during the first term of his administration. In practice the plan is simple. Three days before departure (for example, Wednesday if leaving on a Saturday) is a feast day and proponents of the regimen recommend that extra quantities of high protein food be consumed at breakfast and lunch, and extra carbohydrates at supper. The next day (Thursday in our example) would be a fast day where much smaller quantities of the same types of food would be eaten, protein for breakfast and lunch, carbohydrates for supper. The day before departure (e.g. Friday) is another feast day, and the day of departure is another fast. After resting on the plane, the fast is broken by eating breakfast at the time breakfast is customarily consumed at the destination.

In addition to alternating feasts and fasts, both alcohol and caffeine are manipulated with the jet lag diet. Caffeine is thought to speed up the body's biological clock, and alcohol is thought to slow it down. On eastbound trips caffeinated beverages are avoided in the mornings during the preparatory phase; however, they are considered acceptable for consumption in the evening. The opposite would be appropriate for westbound flights. Alcohol could be used in a manner opposite that for caffeine. This diet is thought to have some biologic plausibility by effecting several of the body's hormonal systems and metabolic pathways.

Motion Sickness

Motion sickness is a common malady which can affect anybody at one time or another. Females appear to be affected more than males; children more than adults. There also seems to be a correlation between the migraine (headache) mechanism and motion sickness. Over-the-counter motion sickness remedies are effective for the majority of travelers and work best when taken before the onset of symptoms. Since there is considerable individual variation in effectiveness as well as associated sedation (the most common side effect), it may be necessary to try several different products to find the best for you. Of the over-the-counter preparations, Dramamine has been shown to be one of the most beneficial.

In severe cases, prescribed preparations are available and often work when over-the-counter products fail. For seasickness, the transdermal scopolamine patches were both popular and effective but, unfortunately, are no longer available. A prescribed remedy, which the U.S. Navy has found to be particularly beneficial at sea as well as in the air, is the combination of Promethazine 25 mg and Ephedrine 50 mg. The recommended regimen is to take one every six to eight hours as needed, with the first dose taken before departure. Since this is available only by prescription, and there are some precautions for its use, consult with your personal physician. A compounding pharmacy should be able to prepare this prescription with little difficulty although the two components can be prescribed, dispensed, and consumed separately.

Certain nonmedicinal maneuvers have proven to be helpful in controlling motion sickness. One is physical location. At sea, for example, mal-de-mer is more apt to occur in a closed off cabin than while on deck. Also, shipboard motion is least pronounced in the middle of the ship and this is where you should be if symptoms get serious. Motion is most pronounced in the bow and stern so these locations should be avoided. In a plane, motion is least pronounced in an aisle seat in a row located at the forward edge of the wing. Some people suggest sitting on the right hand side of a plane on the theory that motion there is less for many flight patterns. On a jumbo jet, motion would be least pronounced in the middle part of each row; however, many travelers develop more symptoms in this section of the aircraft because of narrowed and restricted vision, so be flexible.

If you're prone to motion sickness, don't overindulge in food or drink before or during travel although a light snack may help. Do not smoke, and on a smoking flight, sit at least three to four rows into the non smoking section. Stuffy, poorly ventilated areas should be avoided in favor of fresh air; also peaceful surroundings rather than loud boisterous ones are generally salutary. On a plane, this may mean sitting with the seat reclined as far as it will go, loosening your clothing as much as possible, and aiming the overhead air vent directly at your face. Soft music on the head set may be beneficial.

Symptoms are often worse with the eyes closed or when looking at a close object so trying to sleep or read may be ill-advised. If reading aggravates the condition, try focusing on something far away. Some benefit from looking out the window at the horizon, others don't. When airborne, the drowsiness of anti-motion sickness medication can be accentuated by both the decreased cabin pressure of the aircraft as well as the use of alcoholic beverages, so be careful. Alcohol should be avoided anyway because of its tendency to aggravate motion sickness.

Some less-founded remedies for motion sickness have been popular, including acupuncture and wearing the so-called seasick strap on the wrist. Ginger is a home remedy of long standing for gastrointestinal upset, and it has recently achieved some popularity as an antidote for motion sickness as well as morning sickness in pregnant women. Administered in capsules, the preparation is available at many health food stores. The scientific evidence supporting its effectiveness is weak and why it might work is unknown though it seems to exert its antinausea properties directly in the GI tract rather than in the brain. Ginger does not cause drowsiness, however taken in high doses it can produce confusion as well as gastrointestinal irritation. Try it if you like, but other, more proven preparations would be more likely to help.

If you're tormented by motion sickness, perhaps it will help to know that the susceptibility tends to diminish with continued or repeated travel.

Overland Travel

Motor vehicle accidents are an even greater hazard abroad than they are at home, and constitute the most important threat to the health and well being of the international traveler. Studies of both short and longer-term international travelers, have consistently shown this to be the case.

Many travelers launch themselves into their overseas activities with a thrill-seeking attitude which can interfere with sound judgment and discretion as well as lead to greater risk taking behavior. International travelers are usually not accustomed to the undisciplined drivers often found in developing areas of the world unless, of course, they're from New York City. Foreign locales frequently mean new driving techniques, unfamiliar rules of the road, and strange highway signs. Roads, particularly in developing areas, are not well engineered nor are they adequately maintained. Unique road hazards such as livestock herds, unlit carts and vehicles, makeshift road blocks, and unmarked ditches are common. In many areas, particularly in the evening, a family's living space may very well spill right out the front door and onto the roadway. This is especially true in rural regions.

The magnitude of the risk can vary among foreign locales, and it is difficult to predict where in the world the problem is greatest. As hazardous as driving might be, of even greater concern to the cautious tourist is when the driving is left to someone else. Unfortunately, in many regions, commercial drivers, including chauffeurs, taxi drivers, and bus operators are more frequently involved in ghastly road accidents than drivers of private vehicles. These individuals appear to be more accident-prone for a number of reasons: they tend to be younger and less educated, if not completely illiterate; they often drive under the influence of alcohol and other psychoactive drugs; they manifest more negative attitudes toward safety; and they operate vehicles which are often unroadworthy. Accident rates are higher at nights and on weekends, strong evidence that alcohol is a worldwide factor in highway mayhem.

Some general precautions for the U.S. citizen driving abroad: do not drive more than six to eight hours daily, try to limit a day's drive to no more than 400 miles. Drive defensively; don't insist on your right-of-way. In a high risk setting, a larger vehicle is preferable to a smaller one, and a car is always better than a motorcycle. It has been said that in many areas overseas, the right of **WEIGHT** prevails over the right of **WAY. Always select a car that has safety belts, and always use them.** Unfortunately, safety belts are often flouted, frequently inoperable, and sometimes outrightly rejected as being inconsistent with a cavalier image. Since a very high proportion of accidents occur at night, particularly when returning from a social event, avoid non-essential night driving, don't drink alcohol if you must drive at night and don't drive with those who are obviously under the influence of alcohol or drugs.

International travelers should be familiar with the following: highway rules are often similar to the nautical rules of the road so, if there is no traffic light or stop signs, a vehicle to the right has the right-of-way, even if you are on a main (but not a priority) road. This is not necessarily the case, however, in areas such as the U.K. where driving is done on the left. On the more positive side, in some overseas locales, seat belts are often mandatory for the driver and front seat passenger, and children must sit in the back seat. In such places, any damage awards for injuries sustained in an accident can be dramatically reduced if it can be demonstrated that seat belts were not being worn.

In addition, any time there's reduced visibility, use full headlights. Better yet, use them whenever operating the vehicle. In many areas it is illegal to drive with just your parking lights on (hence the name). Always use directional signals, including before and after passing another vehicle. In many areas this is mandatory, not optional. Overseas, it is common practice, not rudeness, for a driver to sound the horn when overtaking and passing another vehicle. Otherwise, use of the horn is generally reserved for emergencies and not casual/social situations.

Chapter Five

Environmental and Climatic Safeguards

The Tropical Environment

Just as it takes time to adapt to the crossing of many time zones, a period of time is required to adjust to the heat, light and humidity found in tropical climates. The amount of time necessary for adjustment depends on several factors, such as the magnitude and suddenness of the change, the age and health status of the traveler, body weight, level of fitness, and activity level after arrival. Adequate rest, appropriate clothing, a balanced but light diet, sufficient fluids, and adequate salt intake will all help you adjust faster. Individuals who are physically fit adjust faster with fewer symptoms.

It will be necessary, during the first 2-3 days after arrival in a hot tropical location to rest more than usual, performing only essential tasks and avoiding activity as much as possible during the hottest part of the day. Follow the example of the locals: in many tropical regions it is common to work a few hours in the morning and then rest for several hours in the early afternoon when the heat is most oppressive (siesta). Activity may increase to a crescendo in the late afternoon when the temperature is cooler.

Following your arrival in a tropical setting, fluid intake should be appropriate to replace both obvious and water losses of which you are unaware, and to maintain an adequate urine flow. **As a general rule, enough fluid should be consumed to keep the urine dilute and nearly colorless.** If you have a past history of kidney stones, it is particularly important to keep hydrated when visiting a hot climate. When activity is required, a good rule of thumb is to drink a glass of water for every 20 minutes of exertion.

Avoid alcoholic beverages since they can hamper fluid balance and climatic adjustment. Alcohol can actually lead to heat gain in the tropics as well as excessive heat losses in cold, windy, or wet environments. Other substances, including certain medications, can adversely affect the acclimatization process. Fluid pills, for example, can not only aggravate the tendency towards dehydration, but can impair heat transfer to the skin for subsequent dissipation. Antihistamine-containing drugs, such as over-the-counter sleeping aids, allergy pills, and cold preparations, as well as certain tranquilizers and other forms of nerve medication, can affect the heat regulatory centers of the brain and decrease the ability to sweat. **If you are on prescription drugs of any type, review your travel plans carefully with your doctor if any appreciative changes in climate or environment are anticipated, particularly with treks to the tropics.**

Modifying your wardrobe will also help you adjust to a hot environment. In the tropics, cotton is the material of choice. It tends to be loose fitting, light and absorbent. Synthetics, including nylon, should be avoided since this type of material can't 'breathe', lends itself to a variety of skin ailments, and makes the heat more oppressive.

Adjustment involves time, as well as activity and dietary changes. Generally, the older the traveler, the longer this adjustment phase will take. For the first several days after arrival, activities, particularly those scheduled for mid-day, should be kept to a minimum. In addition to resting, you should seek shade, breezes, and air conditioning. Eat lightly and consume appropriate amounts and types of fluids. A slight increase in salt consumption, if medically indicated for you, may prove to be an important adjunct. However, salt consumption is not as critical as water intake, and any increase in salt use must be accompanied by a corresponding increase in fluids. For most sedentary travelers, consuming more salt intake is not critical since the standard diet will contain adequate quantities of sodium. The use of salt tablets is not recommended.

Sun Injury

You can best prevent sunburn by gradual exposure and using sun blocking agents. For almost 20 years, sun tanning/blocking preparations have been rated with a sun protection factor (SPF). The higher the number, the greater the protection. (The number is the ratio of time required for redness to develop with sunscreen compared to the time required for it to develop without it. For a fair-skinned Caucasian in the noonday sun, for example, a barely perceptible redness tends to develop in 15 minutes, so an agent with an SPF of 6 would theoretically protect for 1 to 2 hours (six times longer) before redness develops.) SPF ratings provide only rough guidelines, however, because they were calculated in an artificial indoor environment. Because of the many variables present out-of doors, including indirect exposure to the sun, actual protection is usually considerably less than suggested by the rating. Also, since the products wear and wash off, particularly when swimming or sweating, a cream with an SPF of 15 may more closely resemble a 10. So how do you figure out what's best for you?

Anyone who burns easily should begin with an SPF of at least 15 if not 30. One will still tan, only very slowly. A dark complected individual striving for a deeper tan may utilize an SPF of 4 to help assure against burning. For a sensitive blond with a beginning tan, select an SPF of 8-10. Agents should be reapplied approximately every two hours, and more often if it has become worn off or washed away. The SPF is only one factor to consider; time in the sun is another. Light skinned individuals should not remain in the sun longer than 40 minutes on their first foray to the beach (20 minutes on each side). Each day increase exposure by one-third. **In the tropics the starting time may need to be reduced by up to half depending on complexion.**

High Altitude Syndromes

A variety of clinical syndromes can be caused by exposure to high altitudes (above 6,000 feet) and the resultant stresses imposed by insufficient oxygen. Of these, acute mountain sickness is the least severe, most common, and of greatest interest to the international traveler. Rapid exposure to an altitude in excess of 8,000 feet is enough to produce symptoms in most travelers. These symptoms often resemble a hangover, tend to stop by themselves and, although unpleasant, are usually not serious. They consist of headache, weakness, lassitude, GI distress (nausea and vomiting), dizziness, shortness of breath, loss of appetite, and disturbed sleep patterns. The severity of symptoms varies among individuals and appears to be related to altitude, speed of ascent, duration of stay, simultaneous exertion, and various personal characteristics, including health status. Even though physical fitness is thought to increase efficiency at both high and low altitudes, an exercise program prior to traveling to a high altitude location does not appear to protect the traveler from mountain sickness. It may, however, decrease the severity and duration of the condition.

Because of their potential health hazard, there are a variety of medical conditions which preclude travel to high altitude locations. Many have already been addressed in the sections of this book pertaining to air travel but the following table describes them in terms of travel to higher altitude locations.

TABLE

Conditions Which Preclude Travel to Locations Above 6,000 ft

- Previous attacks of high altitude cerebral or pulmonary edema
- Coronary insufficiency with frequent angina (chest pain)
- Uncontrolled high blood pressure
- Congestive heart failure
- Advanced lung disease, particularly chronic bronchitis and emphysema
- Individuals prone to sickle cell crises
- Recurrent thromboembolic episodes
- Previous retinal hemorrhage

Conditions Which Warrant Specific Assessment Prior to High Altitude Travel

- Mild, stable angina
- Well compensated heart failure
- Controlled high blood pressure
- Recurrent cardiac rhythm disturbance
- Severe obesity particularly with hypoventilation
- Poorly controlled diabetes
- Anemia
- Sickle cell trait
- Retinal disease

Most people will adjust to high altitude locations within a day or two, after which any symptoms should subside. It has been shown that certain medications, if taken prior to ascent, can minimize, if not prevent, mountain sickness. The drug that has been used the most for this purpose is a mild fluid pill known as acetazolamide (Diamox). This medication, known as a carbonic anhydrase inhibitor, finds its primary use in medicine as part of the treatment for glaucoma. When used to prevent mountain sickness, 250 mg dosage is taken three times a day (every eight hours) beginning one to two days before ascent and is continued for one to two days after arrival. Since the drug is a diuretic, careful attention to fluid intake is important. Furthermore, it is also a prescription pharmaceutical and should be obtained only after careful deliberation with one's family physician. Generally, the use of such drugs is unnecessary. For most travelers, it boils down to whether you'd rather awaken at 5:00 AM for several days with a full bladder due to the drug, or a dull headache due to the altitude.

Once encountered, acute mountain sickness is best treated with:

- Rest or limited activity
- Aspirin therapy
- Light meals high in carbohydrate
- Supplemental oxygen, if available
- Time and patience

Nevertheless, in severe or protracted cases, descent to a lower altitude is mandatory. Descent is also advisable for individuals failing to demonstrate improvement of their symptoms after 48 hours. For travelers who have accommodated to a high altitude setting, no problems are to be anticipated upon descent to a destination closer to sea level. The high altitude syndromes appear to be more common in children, suggesting that adjustment is facilitated by age.

It is interesting to note, however, that several recent reports show a tendency for elderly individuals to move away from high altitude locations. Even though this change in residence may be undertaken for health reasons, other explanations have been proposed, including the desire to be closer to specialized medical care, live closer to relatives, in a warmer climate, or in an urban environment.

Chapter Six

Safety Abroad

Important warnings about safety abroad are included in the section on overland travel and issues related to motor vehicle safety. Obviously, motor vehicle mishaps represent a clear and present danger for the international traveler. Two associated risks not previously mentioned which affect longer-term overseas visitors to a higher degree, involve riding in the bed of pick-up trucks and in two-wheeled conveyances such as motorcycles and motor scooters. Even though senior travelers may not be inclined to engage in these activities, they are mentioned since they reflect a very real risk to a broad spectrum of other groups.

In studies of the important medical risks confronted by all overseas travelers, it is readily observed that heart attack is another major concern. There are many stresses associated with international travel and the changes in schedule and activity, which are part of this undertaking, probably amplify the risk. International travel can have an impact on other cardiac risk factors, too. Dietary changes can affect weight and cholesterol, while stress and diet can affect blood pressure. Unfortunately, cigarette smoking is much more prevalent elsewhere than in the United States. This perception of greater social acceptance can adversely affect the ex-smoker, leading to relapse and resumed smoking.

Another serious safety issue, surprisingly, is drowning. Studies of short term travelers, expatriate medical workers, Peace Corps volunteers, missionaries, and peacetime military personnel deployed overseas, show that drowning is a real and persistent threat and common cause of death. There are a variety of explanations to explain this including: unfamiliar surroundings; underwater obstacles; dangerous currents; absence of lifeguard personnel; swimming at night; swimming alone; dangerous marine life; lack of advanced life support services and, perhaps most important, the use of alcohol and other drugs.

To reduce the risk of drowning, specific strategies should be considered. These include not swimming alone; not swimming at night; not swimming in unfamiliar areas that lack beach patrol services; and not swimming after or while consuming alcoholic beverages.

Another safety hazard that is repeatedly identified when studying various overseas populations is the risk of plane crash. The majority of mishaps involve general aviation aircraft rather than commercial aviation services. Of the latter, however, a disproportionate number of incidents involve commuter and non-scheduled carriers and occur at night, in inclement weather, in smaller aircraft, and in connection with smaller airfields. As with drowning, an analysis of the risks helps identify risk reduction strategies. These would include limiting air service to scheduled carriers, utilizing larger jet aircraft, and booking daytime flights.

Safety-related concerns that tend to prey more on the mind of the international traveler are crime and terrorism. Studies of American expatriates dating back 50 years have consistently demonstrated that the risk of violent crime overseas is higher than it is at home. Missionary personnel, for example, are four times more likely to be murdered while serving abroad than they are when home on furlough. Violent crime impacts other international travelers as well. Multinational corporations report that it is increasingly difficult to attract qualified staff for overseas assignments, and one of the most frequently-given reasons is terrorism.

The issues of violent crime and terrorism need to be directly confronted, and again, there are a variety of tactics that can be employed to reduce the risk, both for the expatriate living overseas and the shorter-term visitor. These include such strategies as not driving/traveling alone at night, avoiding reportedly dangerous roads, including those that are isolated and in bad neighborhoods or in known politically precarious regions of a country. Additional guidelines include not wearing expensive jewelry and clothing while abroad, not driving an expensive automobile, and not staying on a strict schedule. If overseas for an extended period, it is best to keep your assets at home. Both expatriates and the longer-term international traveler are advised to maintain contact with embassy and/or consular staff and watch for news of suspicious occurrences in their particular area or circumstances. Other more general recommendations include:

- Leave valuables at home.
- Use only travelers checks or credit cards.
- Do not carry handbags or wear bulky belt pouches.
- Always beware of pickpockets.
- Keep car doors locked while driving.
- Pay very close attention during all monetary transactions.
- If attacked, do not resist. Instead concentrate on the description of your assailant.
- Prepare your tour routes. Do not stand on street corners studying maps.
- Always lock your hotel room and lock valuables in the room/hotel safe.

Substance Abuse

Substance abuse, including alcoholism, can be a major problem from both a medical and legal perspective. It interferes with physiologic and psychologic adjustment to overseas living and contributes to a variety of misfortunes to the international traveler, ranging from motor vehicle mishaps to drowning. It can lead to deterioration in a number of chronic medical conditions and can precipitate or aggravate others, including heat-related illness and diarrheal disease. It can enhance the risk of contracting sexually transmitted disease, including AIDS.

Substance abuse is the leading cause of legal difficulty for the international traveler. Approximately half of the Americans arrested overseas are charged with drug-related offenses, and almost 2/3 of these involve marijuana. There is frequently a false impression that drug use is more socially acceptable in certain foreign locations than it is at home. This is simply not the case. Some countries, in fact, mandate the death penalty for drug infractions while others compel life imprisonment without the possibility of parole. In such circumstances, there is little that U.S. embassy personnel can do to intervene. Drug use, and its mind-altering effect, increases the probability that an international traveler will be the victim of crime.

Finally, as already alluded to with cigarette smoking, international travel can contribute to relapse for people recovering from a chemical dependence problem. It's important to be aware of this risk and guard against it.

Chapter Seven

Food and Water Precautions

Water Purification

Throughout most of the world, you simply cannot trust the quality of the commonly- available drinking water, even when the local citizenry have no problem with it. **ALL** water in less developed regions of the world needs to be treated before drinking or using it for oral hygiene.

Boiling is by far the most reliable method to make water safe for drinking. It should be boiled for five minutes, then allowed to cool to room temperature before using. Do not add ice unless it is prepared from a safe water source. The taste of boiled water can be improved by adding a pinch of salt or by pouring it from one clean container to another several times to aerate.

Chemical disinfection is an alternative to boiling. In the past, chlorine in various forms was the primary agent used for this purpose. However, it is now recognized that its germicidal activity varies greatly with the pH, temperature, and organic content of the water to be purified, and that it is less reliable than other agents. Treatment of water with 2% tincture of iodine is a safe and effective technique that is preferable to chlorine containing compounds. Add 5 drops/quart if the water is clear and 10 drops/quart if it is cloudy or exceptionally cold, then allow it to stand for 30 minutes. With very turbid water, increase the contact time with the disinfectant up to several hours, if possible, prior to use. Adding the iodine will give water a chemical taste, but this is not harmful.

Commercially available water purification tablets containing tetraglycine hydroperiodide (Globaline, Potable-Agua, Coghlan's and others) are also effective. These tablets are usually available at both pharmacies and sporting goods stores. Follow the manufacturer's instructions, and generally double the dose if the water is cloudy. Try to warm ice-cold water prior to treatment. It is advisable to strain cloudy water through a clean piece of cloth to remove sediment and floating material prior to boiling or disinfection.

Adding a powdered soft drink mix to water that has been disinfected with an iodine containing preparation will greatly improve the taste. However, this should only be done **after** the required contact or treatment period since the ascorbic acid in the mix can reduce the disinfecting capacity, and the sugar may facilitate growth of any microorganisms which happen to be present.

Even though it is not common, many people are hypersensitive to iodine and will develop a blotchy red skin rash after drinking it. They are often unable to tolerate many seafood dishes as a result of this sensitivity, and iodine-containing disinfectants are best avoided in such circumstances. Patients undergoing treatment for hyperthyroidism should also use another disinfecting process since the additional iodine could interfere with their therapy and affect metabolic activity.

The various water filters that are available throughout many areas in the tropics (such as Berkenfeld, Metafilter, and Mandler's filters) are excellent at removing many types of foreign matter and for physically clearing turbid water but do not sterilize water or make it safe to drink. Even those filters which contain an iodine resin probably do not adequately disinfect water to the point that it is unquestionably safe to drink. Most filters will remove protozoa and cysts and many will filter out bacterial organisms, but none have a pore size small enough to remove viral contaminants. So, when employing a filtering device, you still need to boil or add a disinfectant to the water.

Since many of the better restaurants abroad share the same concerns over the health risks of impure water, they will often go to some expense to assure the purity of the water they use, or they will offer safe bottled water that can be trusted. Likewise, major hotels in large cities overseas may treat their own water; however, if in doubt, draw a glass of hot water and let it cool. After having passed through a hot water heater, the water has at least been pasteurized and is relatively much safer. Some viruses, such as that responsible for hepatitis A infection, may survive the pasteurization process. Bottled water is widely available, but is bulky and tends to be expensive. Furthermore, it cannot always be trusted since a favorite pastime in some localities is refilling empty bottles at the local hand pump! If, however, you're assured that the water was bottled where the label indicates (an unbroken seal helps), it should be safe for drinking.

Since heating water tends to make it safe, coffee and tea are usually safe beverages for consumption abroad. Make sure the water used in their preparation was first brought to a full boil, and preferably boiled for five full minutes. Freezing water does NOT make it safe, so ice cubes and shaved ice used in drinks should always be suspect. Consequently, the ice served on board aircraft during international flights originating in developing regions should be avoided. Since water is no safer than the container it's in, the traveler should always be suspicious of how glassware, dishes, and utensils have been handled and washed. If they are wet, they should be wiped dry before use. You should be as careful about water for gargling and brushing your teeth as that for drinking. Also, water used for douching should be treated first, if it is from a suspect source. Since many women may find iodinated water irritating to the tissue, it is preferable to treat water for douching by heating and then cooling before use.

This is a rather unusual - even amusing - risk that needs to be mentioned: singing in the shower has been shown to be a risk factor in terms of developing GI disease while traveling! All too often, the showering soprano or baritone realizes that a mouthful of the same water he or she has painstakingly avoided drinking, has just been accidentally swallowed during an aqua-aria.

Other Beverages

Contrary to popular thinking, alcohol will not decontaminate either water or ice, so care must be taken when using either in mixed drinks. Local beers, wines, and soft drinks are generally safe. Avoid draft beer though and order wine only by the bottle. There is a distinct possibility that glasses of beer as well as glasses and carafes of wine might have been diluted with the same water you wish to avoid. For similar reasons, order soft drinks by the can or bottle. The low (acidic) pH of carbonated beverages has long been thought to have an antibacterial quality, but this is only relative.

Locally "processed" milk in less developed areas of the world is never to be trusted because of careless production and inadequate refrigeration. Improper handling, processing, and storage of milk can transmit a wide variety of diseases, including tuberculosis. Overseas, milk of uncertain quality can be made safe by boiling, but this destroys the protein and vitamin D, alters its taste and limits its nutritional value, although the calcium remains intact. Powdered milk is safer and more convenient, providing it is mixed with water from a safe source. Canned evaporated milk is also safe. In developed regions with modern conveniences, pasteurized milk can be considered safe to drink. However, never drink raw milk. For some time the CDC (Centers for Disease Control) has expressed concern over the fad of raw milk consumption which is considered by some to be a health food. Raw milk can be contaminated by salmonella bacteria and other microorganisms. There is just no way to assure that raw milk is safe to drink. Unfortunately, in many areas of the world, there can be no assurances about milk or dairy products in general.

Food Precautions

One of the pleasures of visiting foreign countries is sampling the local cuisine. A few precautions can prevent a gastronomic adventure from turning into a gastrointestinal nightmare.

Nightsoil (human waste) constitutes the main source of fertilizer in much of the world, so it is quite apparent that diseases spread by the so called fecal-oral route can be a constant threat. Eating salads and raw vegetables is a particularly high risk situation. Salads can be made safe if the ingredients are first dropped in either boiling water or are chemically disinfected. If you find these practices aesthetically unpleasant and don't want to do that (and who could blame you?), it is often best to simply avoid fresh salads altogether. Fresh vegetables are safe if they are cooked and eaten hot. Nuts, fruits, and raw vegetables that are peeled, shelled, or skinned before eating, are edible as long as they are purchased intact with no breaks in the shell or skin. However, don't overdo the intake of fruits since this might lead to a diarrheal illness.

All meat and fish dishes should be ordered well done and eaten while hot to eliminate the risk of tapeworm, toxoplasmosis, and trichinosis. Dishes that are highly seasoned or spicy should be suspect since heavy seasoning is a tactic often employed to mask the taste of rancidity and spoilage. Steak tartare, which consists of raw meat, raw egg, and spices is a definite no-no.

As alluded to already, dairy products should be avoided because of the strong likelihood of contamination. In addition to tuberculosis, they can be a source of other infectious agents such as brucellosis. Goat cheese continues to enjoy considerable popularity, but unfortunately, much of that served in Southern Europe and Latin America is also contaminated with the brucellosis germ. Raw eggs should be avoided, even in this country, because they often harbor salmonella.

Remember, refrigeration throughout much of the world, particularly the tropics, leaves much to be desired. Hence it is advisable to avoid dishes that are prepared well in advance and then left to stand. Therefore, stay away from the following:

- Cold platters
- Custards
- Mayonnaise spreads
- Buffet dishes
- Pastries

As if there weren't enough to worry about, further safeguards involve seafood. In addition to the infectious hazards associated with shellfish, there can be various problems with finfish as well. In certain tropical regions, notably the Caribbean and South Pacific Islands, ciguatera fish poisoning represents a significant problem. This is a condition whereby certain reef fish acquire a toxin from the marine environment. As a general rule, when in the tropics, avoid fish which are avoided by the locals as well as barracuda, moray eel, grouper, and red snapper. Don't eat dishes featuring unknown fish.

Markets and menus overseas do not emphasize beef as those in this country do. Instead, such delicacies as camel, goat, horse, iguana, dog, cobra, and shark can be anticipated. Such delights can be tried, but it is advisable to exercise some restraint when experimenting with unfamiliar and exotic dishes. Taste selectively. Stay with toast, tea, and hot soup if you begin to feel queasy. And remember - when strolling the foreign marketplace - **boil it, cook it, peel it, or forget it!**

Restaurant Evaluation

How, overseas, can you tell whether a restaurant is safe? Look for clues (certainly the absence of customers at meal time is a good one). No window screens, open kitchen doors, garbage scattered about, dirt and grease inside, and evidence of insects or rodents are all telltale signs that should suggest avoiding that particular establishment.

Often, the most reliable measure of a restaurant's safety is in the restrooms. Look for absent or poor hand washing facilities, no running water, soap, and hand drying amenities. The absence of any of these is a bad indication, you should assume that the provisions for the food handlers are going to be worse! As disgusting as it sounds, food preparers who can't wash their hands properly are apt to get their feces in the food they're preparing.

The presence of insects, particularly roaches and flies, is an ominous sign. Not only can the bugs contaminate the food, but employees, in their zeal to control the pests, may accidentally, or otherwise, spray insecticide in the food. Some authorities believe that chemical (e.g. insecticide) contamination of food and water in developing countries is just as serious, if not more so, than microbial contamination.

A final pearl of wisdom on the subject of restaurants. If you're in a foreign city and anxious for a restaurant meal, but the appearance of the local eateries leaves much to be desired, try a Chinese restaurant. The meals are generally palatable and wholesome, the food appropriately handled and well-cooked, and the premises adequately maintained. This appears to be reasonably consistent throughout most of the world.

Chapter Eight

Bowel Problems

Travelers' Constipation

Factors leading to constipation in international travelers include the following:

- irregular schedules
- altered eating habits
- diminished fiber intake
- decreased fluid intake
- reduced activity level
- jet lag

Many travelers pack a mild laxative while visiting abroad but care must be taken since you may be more sensitive to medicine during travel. Generally, drinking enough fluids, getting some daily exercise, eating more fiber, taking supplemental fiber preparations when necessary, and judiciously utilizing a stool softening product will suffice to prevent constipation.

Travelers' Diarrhea

Diarrhea tends to be an exaggerated concern among travelers. Actually constipation is more common during international travel (see above).

When diarrhea does occur, it may not necessarily be caused by an infection. Some intestinal upsets are simply a reaction to factors related to travel and may be due to stress, excitement, disruption to your normal routine, unusual food, jet lag, motion sickness, and increased intestinal gas.

Travelers' diarrhea is considered to be an infectious disease and, when it does occur, typically begins 3-7 days after arrival in a new environment, and usually stops by itself, improving in 3-5 days despite therapy. The condition is defined as at least 3 unformed or loose bowel movements in a 24-hour period, together with fluid loss, cramps, bloating and, in some cases, fever, vomiting, and bloody stools. The frequency of travelers' diarrhea among travelers to less developed regions of the world is quite variable, but is often estimated to be in the vicinity of 40%. Reported frequency ranges vary from less than 1% to over 90%, depending on the populations and locations being studied. Among travelers going south of the border to Mexico, for example, the attack rate is thought to vary between 25-50%, accounting for more than a million cases of "Montezuma's Revenge" annually.

Diarrheal illness is much less common with journeys to developed regions of the world, the type of trip the vast majority take. Nevertheless, diarrheal illness can occur with just about any variety of travel, and the affliction is thought to occur in 2-15% of foreign visitors to the U.S. Among visitors to tropical regions, travelers from developed areas such as the U.S. have about a seven-fold greater likelihood of contracting diarrheal disease than people from Third World areas.

However, of greater importance than where one goes or from where one comes is what one eats and drinks. The following table describes foods frequently associated with the development of travelers' diarrhea as well as ways these risks might be reduced. Much of this is a repeat of the food and water precautions already described.

TABLE

Food and Travelers' Diarrhea

High Risk

• Salads, raw vegetables, cold platters, custards and pastries, and other dishes prepared well in advance and left to stand.
• Raw shellfish, raw or undercooked seafood and meat dishes, steak tartare.
• Raw eggs, cheese, milk, and dairy products.

Low Risk

• Raw vegetables if first boiled or immersed in chlorine solution; nuts, fruits and vegetables purchased intact and then shelled, peeled, or skinned.
• Meat and seafood dishes ordered well done and eaten while hot.
• Cooked eggs, pasteurized and refrigerated dairy goods.

Carelessness with water consumption, particularly involving ice cubes, accounts for even greater risk.

Despite the fact that most travelers' diarrhea goes away by itself, it has been estimated that as many as 30% of all cases are severe enough to necessitate confinement to bed for a brief period; and that in another 40%, the condition will be aggravating enough to require some alteration in scheduled activities. Therefore, there is a heightened interest in preventing the problem in the first place.

Rational precautions with food and water form the mainstay of the preventive strategy. **One should not take antimotility drugs to prevent diarrhea**. There is actually some evidence that taking medications which slow GI transit time can increase the risk of travelers' diarrhea. In the past it was popular to take antibiotics to prevent travelers' diarrhea, and considerable research had been conducted on this subject. The first edition of this book outlined certain scenarios where prophylactic antibiotics might be indicated. However, antibiotics for the prevention of travelers' diarrhea are no longer recommended.

The over-the-counter product, Pepto Bismol, has also been found to prevent travelers' diarrhea. Some studies have suggested that it can reduce the risk by as much as 65% when taken for three weeks. Both the liquid and tablet formulations have been tested, and for logistical reasons the tablets are considered to be more convenient. The usual dose is 2 tablets 4 times/day for no longer than 3 weeks. The mechanism of action is not entirely clear, but it seems that bismuth salts (a major ingredient in Pepto Bismol) are not well absorbed and fight microbial activity inside the intestinal tract.

This is not meant to imply that all international travelers should utilize Pepto Bismol to prevent travelers' diarrhea. There are certain risks and side-effects, and the guidance of one's personal physician should be obtained. For example, travelers already on salicylate (aspirin) therapy run the risk of developing toxic salicylate levels on this regimen. This approach should also be avoided by those with a history of aspirin allergy or sensitivity, those with gout, and by travelers on oral anticoagulant (blood thinning) and oral hypoglycemic (diabetic) medications. Side effects include blackening of the tongue and stools.

A pertinent question might then be when is it reasonable to use Pepto Bismol to prevent travelers' diarrhea? The following table, which was originally devised to characterize candidates for antibiotic prophylaxis, can be used to note those travelers who might be considered for this intervention. As a rule of thumb, approximately 20-30% of travelers to developing regions may be candidates for Pepto Bismol prophylaxis.

TABLE

Candidates for Pepto Bismol Prophylaxis Against Travelers Diarrhea

- Business people and diplomats on short-term, very important trips
- Entertainers and athletes on tour
- Military personnel on short-term, strategic assignments
- Newlyweds on honeymoon
- Individuals with an increased susceptibility to diarrhea and those who would be at increased risk if they became dehydrated, such as:
    - Those on certain medications, for example Cimetidine and high dose antacids
    - Those with prior gastrointestinal surgery
    - Certain diabetics on insulin

Should it occur, the treatment of travelers' diarrhea can be considered in the context of four approaches:

- Dietary manipulation
- Oral rehydration
- Antidiarrheal medication
- Antibiotic administration

The first two interventions constitute the cornerstone of management. The diet for travelers' diarrhea varies with the stage of the illness:

- **During periods of active diarrhea:** avoid coffee, alcohol, dairy products, most fruits, vegetables, red meats, and heavily seasoned foods.

• **At the onset of illness:** try consomme, clear soup, salted crackers, dry toast or bread, or sherbet. Yogurt may be tried, but it has few therapeutic qualities. For that matter, neither does lactobacilli, bacteria found in milk now marketed as an alleged diarrhea remedy.
• **As the frequency of diarrhea decreases:** slowly add rice, baked potato and chicken soup with rice or noodles.
• **As stools begin to retain shape:** add baked fish or poultry, applesauce, and bananas.

Adequate and appropriate fluid intake is important with diarrheal illness. Oral rehydration can be an important adjunct in the management of diarrheal disease, and an example of a standard set of instructions follows. Obviously, water for rehydration must come from a safe source, and boiled or carbonated water is recommended.

TABLE
Oral Rehydration

Rehydration Preparations

Prepare 2 separate glasses of the following:

Glass Number 1

Orange, apple or other fruit juice (rich in potassium)	8 ounces
Honey or corn syrup (contains glucose, necessary for absorption of essential salts)	1/2 tsp
Salt, table (contains sodium and chloride)	1 pinch

Glass Number 2

Water (carbonated or boiled)	8 ounces
Soda, baking (contains sodium bicarbonate)	1/4 tsp

Directions

Drink alternately from each glass until thirst is quenched. Supplement as desired with carbonated beverages, water or tea made with boiled or carbonated water. Avoid solid foods and milk until recovery occurs.

There is varying opinion in the medical community about the use of antidiarrheal and antibiotic medications for managing travelers' diarrhea. The use of antidiarrheal agents for the symptomatic treatment of travelers' diarrhea is somewhat controversial. Agents such as tincture of opium (Paregoric), diphenoxylate (Lomotil) or loperamide (Imodium) can relieve the abdominal cramps of travelers' diarrhea; however, when invasive bacteria are the infecting organism, these drugs can intensify the clinical illness and prolong its duration. Kaolin-pectin preparations, such as Kaopectate, alter the consistency of the stool but do not diminish symptoms, the number of bowel movements, or the amount of water and salt loss from the body.

The best advice is not to use antidiarrheal drugs indiscriminantly. Normally, travelers' diarrhea is a way that the body attempts to purge itself of a noxious, toxic, or infectious substance, and a process that should not be inhibited. Use of antidiarrheals should be reserved for occasions such as when:

• Activities or the itinerary will keep one away from lavatory facilities
• Diarrhea is exaggerated and dehydration is occurring
• An important meeting or agenda cannot be interrupted
• Symptoms are severe prior to a long plane trip home

Protracted bouts of travelers' diarrhea can often be stopped with a short course of antibiotic therapy. Because of microbial resistance, certain medications used in the past such as doxycycline (Vibramycin) and the combination trimethorprim and sulfamethoxazole (Bactrim and Septra) are generally no longer effective and are no longer recommended. The antibiotic class known as quinolones has emerged as one with a role in the management of travelers' diarrhea. 500 mg of Ciprofloxacin (Cipro) twice daily for 3 days is a popular regimen, and travelers might discuss with their doctor prior to departure the merits of carrying a supply of Cipro for empiric treatment. The indications for use might be as follows:

• Diarrheal illness clearly getting worse, rather than better after 3-4 days.
• Diarrhea with fever and/or the presence of blood or mucus in the stool.
• Diarrhea sufficiently profound so as to be leading to dehydration.

While on the subject of bowel dysfunction, a new hazard has been identified that is of concern to the traveling public. Many cruise ships, aircraft, as well as other facilities use vacuum toilets. When flushed, a considerable surge of air goes down the discharge pipe along with the contents in the bowl. Individuals, particularly senior citizens, who might be accustomed to flushing the toilet while still seated are at risk of sustaining severe pelvic injury, particularly if the buttocks and thighs completely block the opening to the toilet seat. A syndrome of vacuum toilet evisceration has been described in which the force of the vacuum has actually sucked portions of the intestine out through the anus! Thankfully this appears to be rare, but flusher beware.

It should be stated that it is indeed possible to go overboard in one's attempt to avoid diarrheal illness. Not only can this detract from the enjoyment of traveling and limit the spectrum of activities and cuisine available, but it is amusing to note that **one report in medical literature indicated that diarrhea seemed to occur more frequently the more a traveler tried to elude it!**

Chapter Nine

Other Infectious Diseases

Malaria

Few diseases, if any, have had a greater impact on human social and economic development than malaria. In fact, some have estimated that in a historical perspective, the human toll of malaria is greater than any other cause of death! Despite the publicity given to AIDS, **malaria remains the world's #1 infectious disease, and the risk for international travelers is increasing.** Because of the seriousness and distribution of this disease, the most important medical advice for the international traveler from an infectious disease standpoint is to **take adequate precautions in regions where malaria is prevalent.**

Malaria is a parasitic infection caused by a protozoa known as Plasmodium. There are four species which can produce human disease, and they are transmitted through the bite of an infected female Anopheles mosquito. The disease is characterized by a spectrum of complaints including paroxysms of high fever, chills, anemia, and enlargement of the spleen. One variety of human malaria (Falciparum) is more serious than the other three, and often produces severe or fatal complications.

Transmission of malaria is known to occur in more than 100 countries throughout the world. Over half of the malaria contracted by U.S. citizens abroad was acquired in Africa, and another quarter was contracted in Asia. Of all U.S. citizens traveling abroad for whatever reason, by far the group with the greatest malaria burden has been tourists, with nearly three times the number of cases than were reported in both business travelers and high risk missionary personnel, the groups in second and third place.

Malaria prevention takes two forms: personal precautions to minimize the risk of mosquito bites and prophylactic medications to counter the infecting organism. The latter are to be taken on a regular basis, beginning before and continuing well after the period of exposure. In spite of extensive research devoted towards the development of an anti-malaria vaccine, at the present time all such agents are still investigational.

Personal precautions to minimize mosquito bites include remaining in well screened areas whenever indoors, especially during the hours of dusk to dawn; avoiding aftershaves, colognes, and other fragrant scents; sleeping in air conditioned or well screened rooms or under mosquito netting in unscreened rooms; wearing clothing that adequately covers the arms and legs when outdoors; applying mosquito repellent to clothing and exposed areas of skin when outdoors; and spraying living and sleeping areas with a pyrethrum-based insect spray during evening and nighttime hours. The most effective repellents to be applied to the skin, clothing, and bed netting contain N,N diethyl- metatoluamide (DEET).

The use of prophylactic medication is also important, and in many regions the risk of malaria can be reduced by taking the safe, convenient, and inexpensive medication, chloroquine. Although this medicine technically does not prevent infection, it limits the extent of the infection and suppresses its symptoms. In regions where indigenous malaria is still susceptible to this agent, chloroquine phosphate (Aralen) 500 mg (300 mg base) should be taken once a week beginning 1-2 weeks before entering a risk area, and continuing for 6 weeks after departure. Adults customarily take two 250 mg tablets each dose. This medicine needs to be prescribed, and it is important to specifically discuss possible malaria risk with your physician before embarking on an expedition to a less developed region, even if only visiting major urban centers. Chloroquine should be taken even if the duration of exposure is brief, as short as one evening or an airport stop-over in a malaria zone. Indeed, malaria has been contracted during brief stop-overs in airports within high risk regions, even in passengers remaining on board the aircraft!

Since the drug is started 1-2 weeks before entering a malarious area, your travel itinerary will dictate when the regimen is to be initiated. Ideally, it is helpful to begin dosing prior to departure to confirm that there is no sensitivity to the medication. It is important to stress that the tablets must be taken regularly. Missing one dose can greatly enhance the possibility of contracting malaria, and prophylactic doses of drugs are not normally curative once the infection is established. It does not really matter when chloroquine is taken; however, many travelers find it easiest to remember to take the drug if they take it on Sunday mornings. Knowing a specific day and time to take the prophylactic agent increases compliance and thereby affords greater protection. Chloroquine is well absorbed, even during bouts of travelers' diarrhea.

Unfortunately, chloroquine-resistant strains of Falciparum malaria are known to exist in many parts of the world, and resistance is increasing. Because of this, the medication mefloquine was developed, and it is frequently employed in regions where chloroquine resistance is a problem. Unfortunately, there are contraindications to mefloquine, including an allergy to it or its related compounds, a history of epilepsy, or a history of certain psychiatric disorders. It is important to discuss these issues with your doctor during pre-departure health planning. When it is used, mefloquine is also taken on a weekly basis. Unfortunately, there is a growing problem with mefloquine resistance.

A number of approaches are employed in the face of chloroquine and mefloquine resistance. These may involve the use of such agents as doxycycline and Fansidar, which are available in the U.S., the use of medications available elsewhere in the world (such as Europe) but not yet approved for prescription domestically, or the implementation of other strategies. It is important for the international traveler to remain current with evolving recommendations regarding malaria prophylaxis medications, and the resources described in this text should assist in that regard.

Some travelers may be prone to malarial attacks after they discontinue their prophylactic medications, even when the preventive medicines were taken faithfully. Malaria of the Vivax and Ovale varieties can occur under such circumstances, particularly when there has been a particularly heavy exposure to mosquitoes. Medical attention should be sought promptly in the event of a febrile illness, and the examining physician should be advised of your recent travel history and the possibility of exposure to malaria.

AIDS

The issue of international travel and HIV infection is generally considered in three distinct contexts: HIV screening of international travelers; international travel by HIV-infected individuals and precautions that international travelers should take to protect against HIV infection.

In regard to the first, most authorities concur that HIV screening of international travelers is of no practical value in controlling the AIDS epidemic. Nevertheless, some countries still maintain testing policies. In general this process is being phased out, and where policies do exist, they typically target younger travelers, travelers from less developed regions of the world, and travelers who will be relocating to the host country for a prolonged period of time.

For the most part, this issue will be of little concern to the senior traveler. It is relatively easy through the resources noted in this book to ascertain whether or not screening will be an issue based on one's itinerary. In the uncommon event that screening might be required, such as when establishing longer-term residence in certain developing countries, it is recommended that screening be done before departure rather than after arrival overseas. The results of domestic screening tests are generally accepted abroad; and domestic screening allows for pre- and post-test counseling, the assurance that the injection equipment will be clean, and the benefit that the quality control measures in the testing laboratory will be acceptable.

International travel by HIV-infected individuals raises a variety of issues, and nearly all of them relate to the risks that the travel might impose on the traveler, not the theoretical risks the traveler might impose on others. In this scenario, there are issues related to immunizations prior to departure. For example, live virus vaccines, including that for yellow fever, must be avoided, while at the same time certain other vaccine products, not generally administered to international travelers should be considered. HIV-infected individuals are at greater risk of certain infections abroad and some relatively common ones, such as travelers' diarrhea, can have devastating consequences. Finally, the availability of state-of-the-art health care for AIDS-related illnesses in many regions of the world is either non-existent or sub-standard. Clearly, the HIV-infected individual must be adequately counseled prior to overseas travel.

The main issue of concern to the majority of international travelers is whether their travel might prove to be a risk factor for HIV infection. Despite episodic reports of AIDS being acquired by visitors to highly endemic areas, it is widely accepted that travel, per se, is not a risk factor for HIV infection. AIDS is not transmitted through casual contact, so public facilities, including restrooms, are safe. Much of the concern regarding the latter appears to have arisen from misconceptions regarding the "bathhouse" risk of AIDS within the homosexual community. It was the sexual activities that occurred within the bathhouses, not the bathhouses themselves, that constituted the risk.

In the past there was considerable public anxiety about the possibility of HIV transmission in swimming pools, saunas, and hot tubs if these facilities should become contaminated with potentially infectious body fluids. HIV transmission in such environments must be exceedingly rare if it occurs at all. Nevertheless, it might be prudent for individuals with open cuts, fresh abrasions, or other open sores to avoid crowded, poorly chlorinated hot tubs.

HIV is transmitted the same way worldwide. Casual sex, not casual contact, is the principal risk factor for AIDS. International travel, with its holiday and party mentality and tendency to overindulge in alcohol, can lower one's inhibitions and enhance the possibility of casual sex. Consequently, travel might affect an individual's risk profile. If there is the possibility of casual sex, exercise caution and use protection.

Prostitutes are an important vehicle for HIV transmission worldwide, and in many regions, as many as 90% of prostitutes are HIV-infected. Be particularly wary of swing clubs, escort services, and sex tours. Condoms should be worn for vaginal, anal and oral sex; both men and women who tend to be promiscuous should have ready access to a reliable brand.

Exposure to blood and blood products can be another area of risk. Many travelers go abroad to receive unproven medical "therapies" which are not available domestically. In the process, many receive more than they bargained for, and an excellent example is the so-called "immunoaugmentative therapy" that was provided in the 1970's and 1980's at a private clinic in Freeport, on Grand Bahama Island. Thousands of American cancer patients attended this facility and were injected with a variety of substances, including extracts from necrotic tumor as well as blood from presumably healthy donors and cancer patients. Numerous infections, including AIDS and viral hepatitis, resulted.

Many standard therapies also have inherent risk. Unless it is a life-or-death situation, blood transfusions and infusions of blood products should be avoided when outside the U.S. HIV-antibody screening of the blood supply is not a universal practice, and many foreign countries still use paid donors.

Because so much of the world lacks the resources we take for granted, in many locales disposable medical equipment is often reused. When disinfection and sterilization equipment is unavailable, which is often the cases in developing regions, common procedures such as the injection of drugs and vaccines become much less safe. Globulin products, vaccines, and injectable medications should be avoided in developing areas of the world. The accompanying table recapitulates AIDS avoidance strategies.

TABLE

Precautions for Avoiding HIV Infection and Reducing AIDS Risk While Traveling

DO NOT:

1. Engage is casual sexual encounters.
2. Have sexual relations with prostitutes, members of other high-risk groups for AIDS, or individuals who have multiple sexual partners.
3. Get a tattoo or have body piercing (including ears) when out of the United States.
4. Resort to experimental or acupuncture treatments when traveling abroad.
5. Obtain injectable treatments, medications, vaccines, or gamma globulins in less developed regions of the world.
6. Receive transfusions of blood or blood products when overseas unless it is a true medical emergency.
7. Use illicit injectable drugs or needles and syringes that might have been used previously.

DO:

1. Associate only socially with the indigenous population when traveling, since AIDS is not transmitted by casual contact.
2. Visit local hotels, swimming pools, and restaurants without concern.
3. Use a condom during a spontaneous sexual liaison, and employ such protection during vaginal, anal, and oral sex.
4. Use a spermicidal jelly in addition to a condom during vaginal intercourse.
5. Obtain appropriate vaccines and other inoculations before leaving the United States.
6. In the face of an urgent medical problem or true medical emergency, contact the closest U.S. embassy or consulate as soon as possible. When time is available, staff can advise you of the most prudent course of action.
7. Get the potentially life saving treatment you need when faced with a serious illness or injury. Remember, within the limits of rational judgement, it is better to live dangerously than to die of over-caution!

Emerging Infections

In recent years, a variety of "emerging Infections" have been described, e.g. Legionnaire's Disease and Toxic Shock Syndrome. Of these, a primary area of concern has been the occurrence of Ebola virus infection in the African nation of Zaire. Even though this infectious disease has a reported mortality rate as high as 88% and international commerce and travel have been linked to the disease's emergence, international travelers are not considered to be a target of this virus.

Ebola is only one of several African hemorrhagic fevers (Lassa, Marburg, and Ebola), that are thought to have as their usual hosts a variety of non-human species, principally rodents. In humans, these infections typically begin as fever and muscle cramps and progress to severe illness with respiratory symptoms, severe bleeding, kidney problems, and shock. The range of symptoms can be from relatively mild to fatal. Indigenous populations groups have been the only recognized human target, as indicated, international travelers were not considered to have been at risk, and there were no advisories restricting international travel or activities in the face of the epidemic. No international travelers were infected, not even those integrally involved with study of the epidemic or the treatment of its victims. Therefore Ebola Zaire was, and is, a non-issue for the international traveler. Dengue Fever, however, deserves further comment.

Dengue Fever

Dengue is another viral hemorrhagic fever and one which poses a real threat to international travelers. Like yellow fever, it is a viral disease spread by the Aedes mosquito. Whereas the other more severe hemorrhagic fevers appear to be isolated to specific regions in Africa, dengue viruses are endemic in many countries of the Caribbean, Central and South America (including Mexico), the Pacific, most tropical countries of Asia, and parts of tropical Africa. In general, dengue activity has been increasing in recent years.

Dengue is characterized by the sudden onset of high fever, severe headache, joint and muscle pain, generalized rash, and sore throat. Although the infection is usually self-limited, it can, on occasion, progress to the more severe form known as Dengue Hemorrhagic Fever. This is considered to be quite uncommon among international travelers as recurrent exposure to the virus is thought to be necessary for its hemorrhagic complications.

The risk of dengue to travelers, in general, is low, but visitors to endemic regions should take precautions against mosquito bites. To date, there is no licensed vaccine against dengue. Mosquito precautions have been described in the section on malaria, and it is prudent to apply these precautions whenever visiting tropical regions, even if outside a malarious zone. No specific therapy is available against dengue but, because of its hemorrhagic propensity, both the fever as well as the systemic manifestations are better treated with acetaminophen (Tylenol) than with aspirin because of the latter's anticoagulant properties.

Chapter Ten

Medical Preparedness And Assistance

Finding a Doctor Overseas

With a little planning and forethought, it is usually possible to identify potential overseas health care providers both before departure and when abroad. As already stated, one's family physician and dentist can be helpful sources for referrals or potential leads. As stressed earlier, too, international travelers are urged to join IAMAT and to explore the potential of becoming members of Intermedic. These organizations can be instrumental in identifying overseas providers of medical care. If supplemental health insurance coverage has been obtained, the insurance carrier or underwriter often provides referral assistance, frequently in the form of a MEDEX Directory. If these avenues have been overlooked, the following are strategies to pursue both prior to departure as well as once abroad in order to obtain medical or dental assistance.

Prior to Departure

Contact your local medical and dental societies and the larger health maintenance organizations (the latter regularly develop provider lists for their subscribers). If you're participating in an organized conducted tour, explore resources available through the tour organizer. Students and businesspeople should investigate channels available through their university or employer, particularly if there are ongoing overseas operations, projects, branches, or offices. If you'll be spending extended periods abroad, inquire at the embassy or consulate office of the countries to be visited prior to departure. Contact local medical and dental schools, universities, and religious or mission organizations who have overseas personnel for possible leads.

Finally, particularly for those with a chronic medical condition, explore international services available through professional organizations and disease-oriented societies, such as the March of Dimes, Heart Association, and Cancer Society. By following these recommendations it is unlikely that there will be any difficulty in obtaining assistance; however, the next list describes overseas contacts to consider for help in finding a physician or dentist should the need arise once one is abroad.

Enroute and When Abroad

Most major hotels have a house or contract physician. This is worth remembering even if you do not happen to be staying at a major hotel. In some resort locations such as Acapulco, this may be the only referral source. Contact the hotel's concierge. Americans who live in the country you're visiting can be helpful in recommending sources of medical and dental care. Local medical schools are a reasonable possibility as are the U.S. embassy or consulate office or the overseas office of an American company. Also consider:

- Airlines and steamship companies
- Banks, American Express, other credit card offices
- Tour groups
- Oil companies, and other large firms with extensive multinational activities
- An American overseas mission organization will either have its own medical personnel or a referral system

Less likely contacts for referral would include:

- Local immigration authorities
- Canadian or British embassy or consulate offices
- Canadian or British mission organizations
- The Red Cross
- A Peace Corps unit
- A U.S. military, Air Force, or naval base
- The local public health office
- Any international religious organization
- Any European consulate

Emergencies Abroad

By now you know how to locate a competent physician overseas. However, in the face of an emergency, you may not be in control of who provides initial care or where it is rendered. If there is a choice, and sufficient time, try to get to a hospital affiliated with a local medical school or one sponsored by an international religious organization. **Any major illness or injury that may require extensive and/or prolonged treatment in a foreign locale should be reported to the nearest U. S. embassy or consulate as soon as possible.** This overseas arm of the U.S. government can help refer you for appropriate medical/surgical treatment and provide help arranging for evacuation, should that become necessary. The State Department maintains the Overseas Citizens' Emergency Center, 21st and C Streets N.W., Washington, DC 20520, which assists U.S. citizens who encounter medical, legal, or financial difficulties while traveling abroad. In case of an emergency, the center will direct the inquirer to the nearest U.S. consulate, locate and notify close relatives at home, expedite sending private funds overseas, gather and transmit medical information to overseas physicians, and further assist with medical evacuation. The phone number for the Emergency Center is (202) 647-5225.

An uncommon emergency but one that can be particularly stressful is when an American dies overseas. Should this occur, the closest U.S. embassy or consulate should be contacted at once. Assistance will be offered in facilitating shipment of the remains back home or in arranging burial abroad, whichever is desirable. If, for some reason, the family or close friends are unable to pay for the return of the deceased, burial will take place in a common burial ground in the overseas country. There are no federal restrictions on the importation of human remains as long as the cause of death was not the result of a "quarantinable disease." Since the only quarantinable diseases are cholera, plague, and yellow fever, it is extremely unlikely that a death occurring abroad in a U.S citizen will have been the result of one of these implausible infections. AIDS is not a quarantinable condition.

In the rare event that the cause of death should be attributable to one of the above listed quarantinable diseases, the deceased must be embalmed and then placed in a hermetically sealed casket, or else cremated. Throughout shipment, the remains must be accompanied by a death certificate that has been translated into English and which rather explicitly identifies the body and states the cause of death. An overseas mortician can be of immeasurable assistance in complying with local health department regulations, readying the body for shipment, and in working with the U.S. embassy in finalizing transportation arrangements.

Medical Evacuation

For many medical problems, air evacuation is possible and feasible. Many Americans in certain locations overseas have learned that, in the face of an evolving or urgent condition, the best course of action is to head for the closest airport rather than the nearest emergency room. However, as has already been mentioned, it is often prudent, if not mandatory, to wait a period of time with some medical conditions before entertaining the thought of flying home. Following a stroke or heart attack, for example, the stress and insult of premature flying can have a harmful effect on one's clinical condition.

A person confined to a stretcher does not present a problem in terms of transportation but, if recent surgery were performed or a tight fitting cast is being worn, expeditious air evacuation is ill-advised. Casts should be evaluated prior to flying since cabin pressure changes enroute can produce discomfort and injury to the casted extremity. If a "cast check" raises concern about tightness, the cast may need to be vented prior to departure.

Usually with stable stretcher cases, an attempt will first be made to transport the patient on a commercial flight. Air ambulances and other varieties of private conveyance are generally reserved for more urgent or dire situations. Even with the popular new generation of overseas health insurance packages, when air evacuation is part of the coverage, commercial carriers are typically used. Patients needing transportation as a result of their condition are evaluated by an independent clinician who performs the triaging function. This individual's opinion determines both the necessity for and means of evacuation. Patients cannot dictate the method of transportation.

As a matter of fact, if it is later determined that a special evacuation did not constitute a true emergency, the insurance carrier will demand a supplemental payment amounting to the difference in cost between private and commercial transportation.

Most, but not all, airlines are able to transport stretcher cases if they are given 72 hours advance notice. The extra room to accommodate the stretcher must be paid for by the passenger. Generally, one pays for a maximum of four seats (first-class fare) although up to nine may actually need to be occupied. It is customary for a stretcher case to be accompanied by a qualified escort whose level of expertise matches the needs of the patient.

Chapter Eleven

Retirement and Relocation Abroad

Medical Preparation

As you might imagine, preparation for retiring or relocating overseas involves considerably more planning, preparation, and understanding than a two-week holiday abroad. Most of the previously described recommendations are still valid, it is just necessary to supplement them with additional guidance. Clearly a thorough pre-departure evaluation by one's personal physician is mandatory, including a comprehensive clinical laboratory assessment. The latter should include the following:

- Hematology profile, including white cell differential
- Complete chemistry panel, including lipid profile
- Thyroid stimulating hormone (TSH) assay
- Urinalysis, routine and microscopic
- Prostate specific antigen (PSA) in men over 50
- HIV antibody test if going to a developing area

The health evaluation needs to go beyond the assessment and input of the primary care physician, however. Women should be evaluated by their gynecologist with the evaluation including PAP testing, mammography, and a frank discussion of the issues concerning hormone replacement therapy and follow-up abroad. If under the care of a medical specialist for any reason, an updated assessment from that practitioner should also be conducted prior to expatriation. Complete ophthalmologic and dental updates are also indicated, and all of the above providers should be queried regarding recommendations and referrals.

The earlier chapters of this book commented specifically on some medical conditions that raise serious concerns regarding international travel, if not precluding it altogether. There concerns are heightened in the face of moving abroad. For example, symptomatic cardiac, pulmonary, metabolic, and neurologic disease raise a definite level of apprehension, and in general, should preclude most individuals from pulling up stakes and moving to an overseas locations. Chronic conditions which are generally asymptomatic, but which require regular medication use, are another red flag. These include such conditions as venous stasis, bronchial asthma, diabetes, inflammatory bowel disease, and seizure disorders, to name a few. The availability of knowledgeable sources of medical care and state-of-the-art facilities are generally the issue.

Those who are more seriously ill, including those with AIDS, cancer, or some other potentially terminal illness, should also reconsider their plans, If not for their own sake, for that of their family, friends, and host country. Certainly this decision would be affected by the severity and stability of the condition as well as the location where you are moving, including how close it is to larger metropolitan areas and adequate medical services.

Psychological Issues

It is important to understand both your motives in contemplating retirement abroad and to realize that there will be a difficult period of adjustment once relocated. Both multinational corporations and the U.S. Peace Corps have, for many years, recognized that **somewhere between 25-40% of expatriate staff are unable to complete a two- year tour because of the inability to adjust, and that is after intensive pre-departure medical and psychological screening**. Among the reasons often given were the political climate, including the threat of terrorism; hardships on the spouse and family; and an inability to adjust to the culture.

Culture shock and cultural adjustment must be considered, prepared for, and adjusted to. One must adjust to a new country, a new community, a new neighborhood and, if working, a new job. Collectively and simultaneously; this is a serious challenge if not an overwhelming task. The older the expatriate, the more difficult the challenge. If one is also sick, the burden of this adjustment becomes almost impossible.

For those up to the challenge, having a thorough understanding of the adjustment process increases your likelihood of success. The first stage of the cross-cultural adaptation process is a stage of enthusiasm and excitement. Shortly after an individual arrives in a new country, there is a sense of ardor and fervor which soon result in a sense of being overwhelmed. The newly-arrived person is largely passive at this point in time and, while he or she may feel positive about the new culture, is not yet ready to confront it.

This stage is followed by one of withdrawal and loneliness, as the realization and impact of what one has done hits home. At this point, one is forced to begin interacting with the new culture, which frequently seems strange and unpredictable. There is considerable stress and anxiety, and there may also be growing dislike for the new culture and its people. Disillusionment and criticism prevail as one continues to question the decision of having moved. Somatic complaints are common, including sleep disorders and gastrointestinal symptoms.

Then comes a stage of adjustment and a sense of re-emergence as you develop a better understanding of the situation and become more familiar with local customs. There is a greater degree of comfort with the new culture, its people, and their behavior. People feel less isolated, learn to get around in both the new community and the new country. An important marker of the adjustment process at this stage is regaining your sense of humor.

There may then be a stage of achievement and enthusiasm. Many will actually progress further, not only adjusting to the new culture, but relishing it. Local customs are adopted, including, for example, the local cuisine. The speed of adjustment depends on several things, including the severity of the culture shock, measures taken to deal with it, and the degree of preparation. It does not follow that the more one moves, the easier it is to adapt. Another important factor is whether any so-called "ghosts" come out of the closet. The re-emergency of severe marital discord or a deep depression can severely impact adjustment.

Just as some areas of medical concern speak against international travel, so do those in the psychological and psychiatric area. Again, a history of major depression, particularly if accompanied by suicidal ideology, gestures, or attempts would be a giant red flag. Other warnings would include a history of a major adjustment disorder, a serious problem with interpersonal relationships, and character disorders such as immaturity, instability, personality inadequacy or dependency, and antisocial attitude. As stressed already, any substance abuse disorder, including alcoholism, should be an absolutely clear signal against considering a transnational move. There is some evidence, from studying State Department personnel, that the stresses of cultural adjustment can be a risk factor for the overuse of alcohol, so those with a past history of alcohol abuse or dependence may be at increased risk of relapse when moving abroad.

Much has been said about the psychological side of the equation regarding a move abroad as that has been the primary stumbling block in the adjustment process. There are, however, many thousands of people living comfortable, productive lives overseas. Their adjustment has been successful and their retirement or working circumstances are entirely to their liking. So, while the psychological factors described above are certainly applicable to some and worth reviewing, with a little patience and forethought most people have every reason to believe they can make a similarly happy adjustment to retiring or working abroad.

Conclusion

One of the objectives of this book has been to encourage international travel and give readers the information they need to make such journeys safe, healthy and enjoyable. It stands to reason that, in today's highly mobile society, the prevention, diagnosis, and management of medical concerns is of increasing importance to long and short-term international travelers. The good news is that most health problems associated with travel can be prevented if appropriate safeguards are undertaken before departure, while underway, and after arriving overseas. Other conditions can have their severity and duration reduced by following appropriate preventive measures.

Being prepared medically and emotionally, understanding one's motives, and knowing the hurdles, issues, and risks which lie ahead will go far to make your travel venture a success.

Bon voyage!

APPENDIX I

Resource Organizations of Importance to the International Traveler

Resource Organizations - General

- Access America (Insurance), 6600 W. Broad St., Richmond, VA 23230 (800) 955- 4002
- American Association of Retired Persons (AARP), 1909 K Street, NW, Washington DC 20049, (202) 872-4700
- Department of State Overseas Citizens' Emergency Center, 21st and C Streets NW, Washington DC 20520, (202) 647-5225
- Healthcare Abroad (Insurance), 107 W. Federal St., Middleburg, VA 22117 (800) 237-6615
- International Association for Medical Assistance to Travelers (IAMAT), 417 Center St., Lewiston, NY 14092 (716) 754-4883
- International SOS Assistance (Insurance), 8 Neshaminy Interplex, Trevose, PA 19053 (800) 523-8930
- Medic Alert Foundation International, P.O. Box 1009, Turlock, CA 95380, (800) 344-3226
- Medical Passport Foundation, Inc., P. O. Box 820, DeLand, FL 32721, (904) 734-0639
- Travel Assistance International (Insurance), 1133 15th St., NW, Washington DC 20009 (800) 821-2828
- Travel Guard International, 1145 Clark St., Stevens Point, WI 54481 (800) 782- 5151
- Travel Insurance Pac (Travelers) One Tower Sq., Hartford, CT 06183 (800) 243- 3174
- Travmed (Medex) PO Box 10623, Baltimore, MD 21285 (800) 732-5309
- US Assist (Insurance), 3400 International Dr., NW, Washington, DC 20008 (800) 756-5900

Resource Organizations - Specialized

- George Washington University Rehabilitation Research and Training Center, Ross Hall, Room 714, 230 Eye Street NW, Washington DC 20037, (202) 994-3801
- nternational Diabetes Federation, 3-6 Alfred Place, London, SC1E 7EE, UK, (Worldwide physician directory)
- Moss Rehabilitation Hospital, Travel Information Center, 12th Street at Tabor Road. Philadelphia, PA 19141. (215) 456-9600, TTY (215) 456-9602
- Society for the Advancement of Travel for the Handicapped (SATH), 26 Court Street, Brooklyn. NY 11242, (718) 858-5483
- Specialized Travel Agencies for the Handicapped:
  - Colpitts Travel Sights N' Signs, 450 Providence Highway, Dedham, MA 02026, (617) 326 7800
  - Evergreen Travel Service, Wings on Wheels Tours, 19505 L 44th Avenue W., Lynwood, WA 98036, (206) 776 1184, (800) 435-2288 (outside Washington)
  - Flying Wheels Travel 143 W. Bridge Street. Owalonna, MN 55060, (507) 451-5005, (800) 533-0363 (outside Minnesota)
  - Whole Person Tours, P.O. Box 1084, Bayonne, NJ 07002, (201) 858-3400

Self Help Organizations for Fearful Flyers

- Travel and Fly Without Fear, Inc., 310 Madison Avenue, New York, NY 10017
- The Phobia Society of America, 133 Rollins Avenue, Rockville, MD 20852
- Freedom from Fear of Flying, Inc., 2021 Country Club Prado, Coral Gables, FL 33134

Index

T

V

W

Y

PILOT BOOKS READING SHELF

To order, simply call our toll-free number
(800) 79PILOT

Cruising Canada by Car ... Good Times On a Budget. Take a trip to the foreign country next door. An experienced, enthusiastic and budget-conscious traveler takes you on a motor tour of Canada, province by province. You'll enjoy reading it before you go and use it as a handy guide while you're there. **$8.95**

it's never too late to ... Look and Feel Younger Through Exercise. Senior fitness specialist Olivier Heuts designed the ideal exercise program for today's older adult. Gets great results without strain, pain, an instructor or special equipment! Includes eating tips and relaxation techniques. **$8.95**

it's never too late to ... Understand and Enjoy Casino Gambling by Phil Philcox. Where to go for the most fun and what to do when you get there. Whether you're a seasoned player or just getting started, you'll feel like a pro when you've read this book. **$8.95**

National Directory of Theme & Amusement Parks. Over 550 places to have fun! Broken down by state, this guide features senior citizen and children's discounts; admission fees and specifics on parks' rides, attractions and policy re one price for unlimited use of facility. **$8.95**

the 1997-1998 Directory of Budget Motels. Guide to the best in economy-priced chain motel accommodations in the United States and Canada. Motels meet rigid quality standards and are convenient to major highway systems. Includes motel headquarter listings for more information, many with toll free 800 numbers. **$8.95**